Python 3 Image Processing
Learn Image Processing with Python 3, NumPy, Matplotlib, and Scikit-image

By

Ashwin Pajankar

Distributors:

BPB PUBLICATIONS
20, Ansari Road, Darya Ganj
New Delhi-110002
Ph: 23254990/23254991

BPB BOOK CENTRE
376 Old Lajpat Rai Market,
Delhi-110006
Ph: 23861747

MICRO MEDIA
Shop No. 5, Mahendra Chambers,
150 DN Rd. Next to Capital Cinema,
V.T. (C.S.T.) Station, MUMBAI-400 001
Ph: 22078296/22078297

DECCAN AGENCIES
4-3-329, Bank Street,
Hyderabad-500195
Ph: 24756967/24756400

Published by Manish Jain for BPB Publications, 20, Ansari Road, Darya Ganj, New Delhi-110002

Dedicated To

Dr Vijay Bhatkar

Architect of India's first Supercomputer, PARAM

Preface

The author is confident that the present work in form of this book will come as a relief to the students, makers, and professionals alike wishing to go through a comprehensive work explaining difficult concepts related to Image Processing, the scientific Python ecosystem, and scikit-image in the layman's language. The book offers a variety of practical image processing programs with scikit-image. Also, this is the one of the very first printed books on the area of image processing that offers detailed instructions on scikit-image and Jupyter notebook combination.

This book promises to be a very good starting point for complete novice learners and is quiet an asset to advanced readers too. The author has written the book so that the beginners will learn the concepts related to scientific Python ecosystem and image processing in a step-by-step approach.

Though this book is not written according to syllabus of any University, students pursuing science and engineering degrees (B.E./B.Tech/B.Sc./ M.E./M.Tech./M.Sc.) in Computer Science, Electronics, and Electrical streams will find this book immensely beneficial and helpful for their projects and practical work. Software and Information Technology Professionals who are beginning to learn scientific computing or want to switch their careers to computer vision will also benefit from this book.

It is said *"To err is human, to forgive is divine"*. In this light the author wishes that the shortcomings of the book will be forgiven. At the same time, the author is open to any kind of constructive criticisms, feedback, corrections, and suggestions for further improvement. All intelligent suggestions are welcome and the author will try his best to incorporate such in valuable suggestions in the subsequent editions of this book.

Acknowledgement

No task is a single man's effort. Cooperation and Coordination of various peoples at different levels go into successful implementation of this book.

There is always a sense of gratitude, which everyone expresses to the others for the help they render during difficult phases of life and to achieve the goal already set. It is impossible to thank individually but I am hereby making a humble effort to thank and acknowledge some of them.

I would like to thank **Mr. Manish Jain** for giving me an opportunity to write for BPB Publications. Writing for BPB has been my dream for me for last 15 years as I grew up reading books authored by Yashavant Kanetkar. I have published more than a dozen books with the publishers around the globe till now and this is my third book for BPB Publications.

Finally, I want to thank everyone who has directly or indirectly contributed to complete this authentic piece of work.

About the Author

Ashwin Pajankar is a polymath. He has more than two decades of programming experience. He is a Science Popularizer, a Programmer, a Maker, an Author, and a Youtuber. He is passionate about STEM (Science-Technology-Education-Mathematics) education. He is also a freelance software developer and technology trainer. He graduated from IIIT Hyderabad with M.Tech. in Computer Science and Engineering. He has worked in a few multinational corporations including Cisco Systems and Cognizant for more than a decade.

Ashwin is also an online trainer with various eLearning platforms like BPBOnline, Udemy, and Skillshare. In his free time, he consults on the topics of Python programming and data science to the local software companies in the city of Nasik. He is actively involved in various social initiatives and has won many accolades during his student life and at his past workplaces.

Table of Content

Preface   v

Acknowledgements   vii

1. Concepts in Image Processing...1
   1.1   Signal and Signal Processing 1
   1.2   Images and Image Processing 2
   1.3   Summary 3
         Exercise 3

2. Installing Python 3 on Windows 5
   2.1   Python Website 5
   2.2   Summary 8
         Exercise 8

3. Introduction to Raspberry Pi..9
   3.1   Single Board Computers 9
         3.1.1   Advantages and Disadvantages of Single
                Board Computers 11
         3.1.2   Popular SBC Families...............................12
   3.2   Raspberry Pi 14
   3.3   Raspbian Operating System 17
   3.4   Setting Up and Booting a Raspberry Pi 17
         3.4.1   Hardware Required for Setup....................17
         3.4.2   Software Required for Setup 20
         3.4.3   Write OS to Microsd Card.........................22
         3.4.4   Boot up the Pi..24
   3.5   config.txt and raspi-config...25
   3.6   Connect to Network 28
         3.6.1   Connect to WiFi 28
         3.6.2   Connect to Wired Network.........................29
         3.6.3   Check the Status of Connection 30
   3.7   Remote Connection to Raspberry Pi 31

	3.7.1	Accessing Command Prompt with PuTTY and Bitwise SSH Client	31
	3.7.2	Remote Desktop with RDP and VNC	34
3.8	Updating Raspberry Pi		38
3.9	Shutting Down and Restarting Raspberry Pi		38
3.10	Why to use Raspberry Pi		39
3.11	Summary		39
	Exercise		39

4. Python 3 Basics 41
4.1	History of Python Programming Language	41
4.2	Why Python 3	42
4.3	Features and Benefits of Python Programming Language	42
4.4	IDLE and Hello World!	44
4.5	Python Interpreter Mode	47
4.6	Python on Raspberry Pi Raspbian OS	48
4.7	Other editors in the Raspbian	49
4.8	Summary	51
	Exercise	51

5. Introduction to the Scientific Python Ecosystem 53
5.1	Python Package Index (PyPI) and pip	53
5.2	Scientific Python Ecosystem	54
5.3	IPython and Jupyter	55
5.4	Summary	62
	Exercise	62

6. Introduction to NumPy and Matplotlib 63
6.1	Introduction to NumPy		63
	6.1.1	Ndarray	63
	6.1.2	Installation of NumPy and Matplotlib	64
6.2	Getting Started with NumPy Programming		64
6.3	Ndarray Properties		67
6.4	Ndarray Constants		68
6.5	Ndarray Creation Routines		68
6.6	Ndarray Creation Routines with Matplotlib		70
6.7	Random Data Generation		75
6.8	Array Manipulation Routines		75

6.9   Bitwise and Statistical Operations....................................81
6.10   Summary 82
        Exercise 82

7. Visualization with Matplotlib...83
7.1   Single Line Plots 83
7.2   Multiline Plots 85
7.3   Grid, Axes, and Labels 88
7.4   Colors, Styles, and Markers 93
7.5   Summary 99

8. Basic Image Processing with NumPy and Matplotlib...............101
8.1   Image Datasets 101
8.2   Installing Pillow 102
8.3   Reading and saving images 102
8.4   NumPy for Images 104
8.5   Image Statistics 106
8.6   Image Masks 106
8.7   Image Channels 107
8.8   Arithmetic Operations on Images 109
8.9   Bitwise Logical Operations 111
8.10   Image Histograms with NumPy and Matplotlib 112
8.11   Summary 114
        Exercise 114

9. Advanced Image Processing with NumPy and Matplotlib.......115
9.1   Color to Greyscale Conversion 115
9.2   Image Thresholding...116
9.3   Tinting Color Images...119
9.4   Shading Color Images 120
9.5   Gradient...120
9.6   Max RGB Filter...121
9.7   Intensity Normalization..121
9.8   Summary 122
        Exercise 122

10. Getting Started with Scikit-Image...123
10.1   Introduction to Scikits 123

10.2 Installation of Scikit-learn on Windows and
Raspberry pi Raspbian 123
10.3 Basics of Scikit-image... 124
10.4 Colorspace Conversion 125
10.5 Summary 126
   Exercise 126

11. Thresholding Histogram Equalization and Transformations.. 127
11.1 Simple Thresholding, Otsu's Binarization, and
Adaptive Thresholding 127
11.2 Histogram Equalization.. 130
11.3 Image Transformations... 131
11.4 Summary 137
   Exercise 137

12. Kernels, Convolution and Filters... 139
12.1 Image Filtering 139
12.2 Built-in Image Filters in Scikit-image.......................... 143
12.3 Summary 147
   Exercise 147

13. Morphological Operations and Image Restoration 149
13.1 Mathematical Morphology and
Morphological Operations.. 149
13.2 Image Restoration by Inpainting 153
13.3 Summary 156

14. Noise Removal and Edge Detection... 157
14.1 Noise 157
14.2 Noise Removal 159
14.3 Canny Edge Detector 161
14.4 Summary 162
   Exercise 162

15. Advanced Image Processing Operations................................. 163
15.1 SLIC Segmentation 163
15.2 Tinting Greyscale Images... 164
15.3 Contours 165
15.4 Summary 166

16. Wrapping Up **167**

    16.1   Python Implementation and Distributions......................... 167

    16.2   Anaconda... 167

    16.3   Conda Package Manager... 168

    16.4   Spyder IDE... 169

    16.5   Summary 170

    16.6   Conclusion.. 170

CHAPTER 1
Concepts in Image Processing

I hope that you have read the preface and the table of contents thoroughly. If not, I recommend you to read them so that you will have an idea of the things that you can expect in this chapter and in the entire book. This being the first chapter of the book, is mostly an informative chapter and we will be learning a lot of important concepts for the topics we will see in this book. The programming hands on and other things will be there in the subsequent chapters. So, let us start the exciting journey of image processing by learning few important concepts.

1.1 Signal and Signal Processing

A fluctuating quantity that conveys information is known as a **Signal**. This is the scientific definition of signal. In our day to day life, we come across various types of signals like human gestures and TV/radio signals. All these signals convey some type of information to the recipients. Essentially, signals represent information.

Signal Processing is a scientific discipline that includes analysis of signals and extracting useful information from signals. Signal processing is a sub-discipline of Mathematics, Information Systems, and Electrical Engineering. The following Venn diagram shows us the relationship between all the disciplines mentioned above. *(figure 1.1)*

The system or the entity that carries out the task of processing signals is a **Signal Processing System**. The most prominent example of a signal processing system is a radio set that converts radio signals into audible signals. I prefer to classify the signal processing systems into naturally occurring signal processing systems (for example eyes) and man-made signal processing systems (like TV or radio). A man-made signal processing system that is made of electronic components is known as **Electronic Signal Processing System**. It is further classified into two types based on the nature of signals it processes, and electronic signal processing system can either be analog or digital.

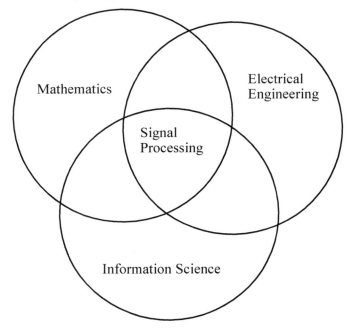

Figure 1.1   Venn diagram for Signal Processing

We know that the analog signals are continuous and digital signals are discrete in nature. There are many more differences to the analog signals and digital signals. It is an interesting exercise to find out the difference between them.

1.2 Images and Image Processing

An **image** is a signal. The entity that processes images is an **Image Processing System**. It can be a natural system like eye and brain pair or man-made system. We can further classify man-made image processing systems into analog image processing systems and digital image processing systems.

A **film camera** or **a motion picture** camera is an analog image processing system where the picture is stored in the film which is an analog format. A film projector is also an example of an analog signal processing system. A digital camera and a computer are good examples of digital image processing systems. In the digital image processing, the images are captured and processed in the digital format. Digital image storage formats use digital bits (0s and 1s) to represent images. The digital images are stored in the digital storage mediums like optical storage (CD, DVD), semiconductor storage (SSD), or magnetic storage (tapes).

Image processing has applications in the following areas:

- Image sharpening and restoration
- Medical image processing
- Remote sensing
- Transmission and encoding of information
- Machine and Robot vision
- Pattern recognition and artificial intelligence
- Video processing
- Astronomy
- Computer graphics
- Spectroscopy

1.3 Summary

In this very short chapter, we have learned a few important concepts that we are going to see in details in the subsequent chapters of the book. In the next chapter, we will see the process of installation of Python 3 on the windows.

Exercise

As an exercise to this chapter, you can find out the more differences between analog and digital signals.

CHAPTER 2
Installing Python 3 on Windows

In the last chapter, we had a brief overview of the definitions of the important concepts that we will be discussing in this book. This chapter is dedicated to understanding the installation process of Python 3 on Windows computer and setting up the environment for programming.

2.1 Python Website

We can visit Python website to download the installable for Windows platform. The URL to the Python website is www.python.org. Open any web browser of your choice and visit this URL. The following page will appear in the browser windows: *(figure 2.1)*

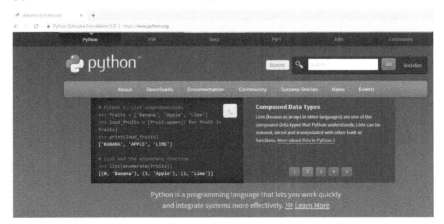

Figure 2.1 Python Homepage

The page shown above in *figure 2.1*, is Python's homepage. There is a **Downloads** link in the horizontal menu. Hover the mouse pointer over the Downloads link and following popup will appear: *(figure 2.2)*

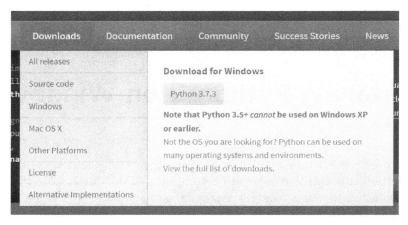

Figure 2.2 Download for Windows

Based on your operating system, it will show you the appropriate download option. For Windows, it will be an executable installation file. At the time of writing this book, the most recent version is 3.7.3 and by the time you are reading this, it might have had new release already. But the concepts and programming examples in this book will mostly be the same. So, go ahead and download the file. Once the download finishes, you can find the **python-3.7.3.exe** in **Downloads** directory of your user. Once located, double click on it, to start installation process. Following window will appear: *(figure 2.3)*

Figure 2.3 Python 3 installation

Make sure to check all the checkboxes. The last checkbox will make sure that we can launch the Python 3 executable from the command prompt. Then, click **Install Now**. It will ask you for admin privileges. After that it will continue the installation process and once the installation is successful, it will show the following window, *(figure 2.4)*

Figure 2.4 Python 3 installation success

You can click **Close** button and installation window will close. The Python 3 interpreter and **Integrated Development and Learning Environment (IDLE)** has been installed.

You can find the Python 3 interpreter and IDLE by searching in the search box of Windows. Another way to verify is to open **cmd** program and type in the command *python* at the command prompt. It should invoke the Python 3 interpreter as shown in *figure 2.5.*

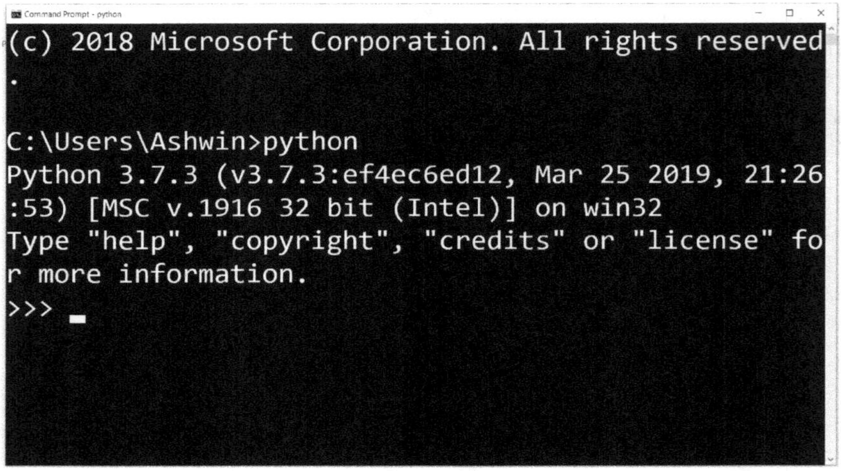

Figure 2.5 Python 3 interpreter on Windows cmd

Note that the above step is only possible if you checked the checkbox asking you to add python to *PATH* during installation. To exit you need to type the command `exit()` and press enter.

2.2 Summary

In this chapter, we had learned to install the python interpreter on a Windows computer. We have not covered anything about the python basics and programming yet because we will study those concepts in the dedicated chapters. In the next chapter, we will see the Raspberry Pi and its setup in detail.

Exercise

As an exercise to this chapter, explore the homepage of python, www. python.org.

## CHAPTER 3

Introduction to Raspberry Pi

In the last chapter, we learned how to install Python 3 on windows. We also saw how to verify the environment and also explored Python Software Foundation's website www.python.org.

In this chapter, we will familiarize ourselves with the concept of **Single Board Computers**. Then we will explore Raspberry Pi, the most famous Single Board Computer of our generation, in detail. We will learn how to boot up **Raspberry Pi** with **Raspbian OS**. Then, we will proceed to connect the Pi with the outside world through internet. We will learn how to remotely access Raspberry Pi Raspbian desktop and command prompt. In addition to that, we will also study hardware specifications of Raspberry Pi's latest model.

3.1 Single Board Computers

A **Single Board Computer (SBC)** is a complete functional computer on a single **printed circuit board (PCB)**. The PCB of a SBC has all the components like microprocessor, input/output ports, memory, and Ethernet port/WiFi that is needed for a full-fledged working computer. SBCs can be used for variety of purposes including learning how to write programs, building a NAS drive, robotics, and home automation, and performing home computing tasks like web browsing or word processing or spreadsheets.

SBCs were originally developed for providing easy access to programming platforms for those who could not afford big computers. In the era of 70s, 80s, and 90s, before the rise of Desktop/Personal computers, the market was dominated by home computers which, basically, were SBCs.

The first true single-board computer called the "*dyna-micro*" used the Intel C8080A as CPU. It also used Intel's first EPROM, the C1702A. The dyna-micro was re-branded by **E&L Instruments** in 1976 as the *MMD-1* **(Mini-Micro Designer 1)**. You can find more information about MMD-1 at http://www.decodesystems.com/mmd1.html. Following is a photograph of an early prototype of MMD-1, *(figure 3.1)*

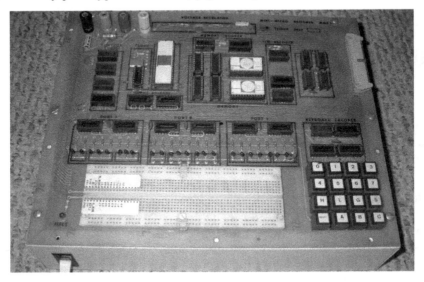

Figure 3.1 An early prototype of MMD-1

One of the earliest famous and widely sold home computer was BBC Micro. Following is a photograph of BBC Micro, *(figure 3.2)*

Figure 3.2 BBC Micro

As the technology progressed, the new era of low-cost desktop computers began with IBM PC and home computers gradually faded into obscurity. However, with the advent of new technologies like **Universal Serial Bus (USB)** and advances in semiconductor fabrication technology, there is resurgence of SBCs once again. Due to the usage of **System on a Chip (SoC)**, the sizes of SBCs have been drastically reduced to the size of a credit card. A SoC is an **integrated circuit (IC)** that has all the components like microprocessor, memory, and I/O on a single chip. A popular example of SoC, apart from SBCs, is mobile computing devices like mobile phones and tablets. SoCs are also used in embedded systems and **Internet of Things (IoT).**

SBCs, in the form of home computers, were originally envisioned to be targeted for education sector and to provide access to programming platforms to students. However, they have found applications in the industry, research and industries like IoT (Internet of Things) actively use SBCs due to their compact size.

3.1.1 Advantages and Disadvantages of Single Board Computers

While discussing SBCs, we must discuss their advantages and disadvantages. We know that the SBCs have all the components required for a functional computer on a single PCB. This helps to reduce the size. Most of the very popular SBCs are of the size of a credit card and can easily fit in the breast pocket of a shirt or pockets of men's trousers. This is the most significant advantage of SBCs as due to small size, they can be used in embedded applications and Internet of Things projects. Small size also optimizes (in this case, reduces) the cost of production per unit. Thus, there are dozens of SBCs with price tag of less than 100 USD.

Due to the constraint of the size, the SBCs cannot pack significant computing power. SBCs are good enough for home computing, web browsing, IoT, Industrial, and Embedded but not for the tasks that are computationally expensive. Also, due to the fact that all the components are on a single PCB, it is not possible to upgrade individual component. In the desktop computers, it is possible due to the modularity of the components. Also, if any component of SBC is damaged, then, due to the same lack of modularity, it is not possible to replace it easily.

3.1.2 Popular SBC Families

Let us have a look at a few popular and low-cost SBC families.

Raspberry Pi is a very popular family of credit card sized single board computers. We will see that in the coming sections.

Another popular family of popular single board computer is Banana Pi and Banana Pro. *(figure 3.3)*

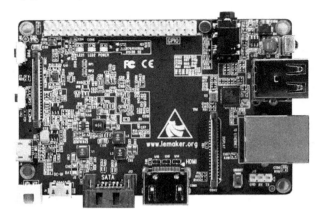

Figure 3.3 Banana Pro

Intel also had Intel Edison and Galileo boards which have been discounted. It has introduced a new platform as of 2019 which is called UP Squared. *(figure 3.4)*

Figure 3.4 UP Squared by Intel

Asus also has launched a SBC known as Tinker Board. *(figure 3.5)*

Figure 3.5 ASUS Tinker Board

Even Arduino, which is a popular family of programmable microcontrollers, has many SBCs like Arduino Tian, *(figure 3.6)*

Figure 3.6 Arduino Tian

3.2 Raspberry Pi

Raspberry Pi is a series (or family) of single board computers that are very popular. In fact, many people attribute the contemporary resurgence of popularity of SBCs to Raspberry Pi. Raspberry Pi Foundation and Raspberry Pi Trading manage the Raspberry Pi brand. Eben Upton is the brain behind the Raspberry Pi and currently serves as the CEO of Raspberry Pi Trading. He is responsible for Software and Hardware architecture of Raspberry Pi series.

The first generation of Raspberry Pi, known as **Raspberry Pi 1 Model B**, was released in February 2012 and it became a great commercial success. In fact, Raspberry Pi is the most sold British computer. Since then, many more models of Raspberry Pi have been released.

As of April 2019, the latest member of Raspberry Pi series is **Raspberry Pi 3 Model B+**. Following are the specifications of Model B+,

Soc	Broadcom BCM2837B0
CPU	4 × Cortex-A53 1.4 GHz
FPU	VFPv4 + NEON
GPU	Broadcom VideoCore IV (3D part of GPU @ 300 MHz, video part of GPU @ 400 MHz)
Memory	1 GB RAM shared with GPU
Networking Options	Ethernet Port and WiFi
USB 2.0 Ports	4
Production status	Will be in production till 2023

The information given above is quite useful when using Raspberry Pi for image processing programing examples in this book. Raspberry Pi has a few other features like **GPIO Pins** that are outside the scope of this book.

Following is the photograph of the top view of **Raspberry Pi Model 3 B+**, *(figure 3.7)*

Figure 3.7 Raspberry Pi 3 Model B+ top view

In the *figure 3.7*, at the top left, we can see the GPIO pins. At the bottom left, we can see the micro USB port for the power supply. Adjacent to that is the HDMI video output port. At the right hand side, we have USB and Ethernet ports. We will be using these ports only throughout the book. Following *figure 3.8,* is the image with a better look at the Ethernet and four USB 2.0 ports,

Figure 3.8 Raspberry Pi 3 Model B+ Ethernet and USB 2.0 ports

Figure 3.9, gives us a nice look at all the I/O ports and power port of the Pi,

Figure 3.9 Raspberry Pi 3 Model B+ ports

Figure 3.10 is the bottom view of the Pi with the slot for microSD card clearly visible,

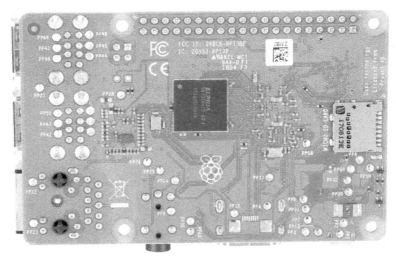

Figure 3.10 Raspberry Pi 3 Model B+ bottom view

At the left-hand side of figure 3.10, we can clearly see the slot for microSD card.

You can find more information about the specifications of other models of Raspberry Pi at https://www.raspberrypi.org/products/.

3.3 Raspbian Operating System

Raspberry Pi is capable of running many Operating Systems including Raspbian (we will see this in detail), Ubuntu, and Windows 10 IoT Core. Raspbian is the official operating system of Raspberry Pi. It is a variant of the Debian, which is a popular Linux distribution itself, optimized for Raspberry Pi hardware. For beginners, it is recommended to download the Raspbian image available at the downloads page of Raspberry Pi foundation, https://www.raspberrypi.org/downloads/raspbian/. You can find more details of Raspbian project at their homepage https://www. raspbian.org.

3.4 Setting Up and Booting a Raspberry Pi

Let's setup and boot the Raspberry Pi.

3.4.1 Hardware Required for Setup

We will see the list of hardware components required for the Raspberry Pi Setup.

- **Raspberry Pi Board**

  I am using a Raspberry Pi 3 Model B+ Board. The instructions for the setup are more or less same for all the models. If there is anything different, then I will mention in the instructions.

- **A Windows Computer**

  You need to have access to a Windows desktop or laptop. We can use Linux or Mac too. However, most of the readers are comfortable with Windows and I want to keep it very simple.

- **Keyboard and Mouse**

  We need a pair of USB keyboard and mouse to connect to the Pi.

- **Internet connection**

  We also need a high-speed internet (WiFi or Ethernet) for downloading the software.

- **microSD card**

  A microSD card of minimum 8 GB of storage is a must. I prefer using a class 10 microSD card of 16 GB storage. It acts as the secondary storage for the Pi. We will install Raspbian OS in this microSD card. *(figure 3.11)*

Figure 3.11 An 8 GB microSD card

- **Power supply**

  Raspberry Pi requires 5 volts of power supply. It is recommended that it should be of 2.5 amps, so that it can work with any model of Raspberry Pi. Remember that Raspberry Pi needs a micro USB type for power. You can find Raspberry Pi Universal Power Supply at https://www.raspberrypi.org/products/raspberry-pi-universal-power-supply/. It will work for all the models of Raspberry Pi. *(figure 3.12)*

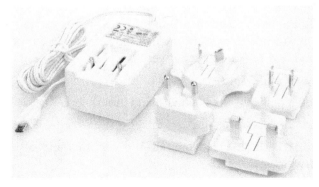

Figure 3.12 Raspberry Pi Universal Power Supply

- **Card Reader and microSD to SD card converter**

  Many laptops come with built in SD card readers. If you do not have a built-in card reader in your computer, you need a card reader as shown in *(figure 3.13)*,

Figure 3.13 Memory card reader

  If you have an older model of Pi like Pi 1 Model B, then you need a microSD to SD card converter, *as shown in figure 3.14,*

Figure 3.14 Memory card Adapter/Converter

- **Monitor**

  We can use a HDMI monitor for visual display. For that we need a HDMI male-to-male cable. Following is an image of HDMI male connector, *(figure 3.15)*

Figure 3.15 HDMI Male Port

If you are planning to use a VGA monitor then you will need VGA male-to-male connector, *(figure 3.16)*

Figure 3.16 VGA male-to-male connector

With VGA monitor and male-to-male cable, we also need HDMI-to-VGA signal converter, *(figure 3.17)*

Figure 3.17 HDMI-to-VGA signal converter

This is the entire list of the hardware required for the setup and first boot of a Raspberry Pi board.

3.4.2 Software Required for Setup

We know that the microSD card acts as the storage for the Pi and the Raspbian OS is written onto the card. There are two ways to write the OS on the card. The first one is **New Out Of the Box Software (NOOBS)**. I am not discussing NOOBS in this book as I believe that manually writing the OS to the card gives you the opportunity to change the settings in case you need it that way. In this section, we will see how to tweak the settings in the microSD card manually. So let's understand how to prepare the microSD card manually. For that we need to download the free software that is required to prepare the microSD card.

- **Download Raspbian OS image**

  Open the browser and visit https://www.raspberrypi.org/downloads/ raspbian/. Following page will appear, *(figure 3.18)*

Figure 3.18 Various Raspbian OS images

There are 3 options. Out of those download the zip file for **Raspbian Stretch with desktop and recommended software**. This image will have all the required softwares needed for our image processing programming exercise and we will get a full desktop and won't have to install a lot of softwares afterwards.

- **WinZip or WinRaR**

  The image is in the zip format which is compressed format. We have to download an extraction software like WinZip or WinRaR. So, download it from https://www.winzip.com or https://www.win-rar. com. Once you download and install the software, extract the image file.

- **Win32 Disk Imager**

  The extracted image will be an ISO format file. It has to be written to the microSD card. For that we need to download and install Win32 Disk Imager from https://sourceforge.net/projects/win32diskimager/.

3.4.3 Write OS to Microsd Card

Once Win32 Disk Imager is installed, we are ready to write the ISO image on the microSD card. Insert the microSD card into the card reader and connect it to the computer / laptop. Wait for some time till the computer detects the card. It will show it as a new disk. Open Win32 Disk Imager. The window will look as shown in figure 3.19,

Figure 3.19 Win32 Disk Imager

Choose the appropriate disk from the Device dropdown. If you choose the wrong disk then it will overwrite the data in that disk. So, be careful while choosing the disk. After choosing the disk, choose the extracted ISO file from for the **Image File** section by clicking the blue folder icon. This will enable the **Write** button. Click the Write button. If the write protection notch is turned on then following error window will appear, *(figure 3.20)*

Figure 3.20 Win32 Disk Imager

Toggle the write protection notch. Then, click the write protection button again. This will allow us to write the ISO file to the microSD card. However, before we can continue, it will show a warning message like the one shown in *figure 3.21*,

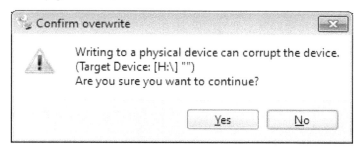

Figure 3.21 MicroSD card overwrite warning message

Clock the **Yes** button to continue. It will start writing the data to the microSD card. Once the data writing is finished, following message will appear, *(figure 3.22)*

Figure 3.22 Success message

The Raspbian OS image has been written to the microSD card.

3.4.3.1 Alter the contents of config.txt for VGA monitors

If you are planning to use VGA monitor then we need to change config.txt file. Disconnect the microSD card reader from the computer and connect it again. It will appear as a new drive named as **boot**. This is the boot partition of Raspbian OS. Only this partition is accessible to the Windows when the microSD card is read. Now, we need to make the following changes to the `config.txt` file.

1. Change #disable_overscan=1 to disable_overscan=1
2. Change #hdmi_force_hotplug=1 to hdmi_force_hotplug=1
3. Change #hdmi_group=1 to hdmi_group=2
4. Change #hdmi_mode=1 to hdmi_mode=16
5. Change #hdmi_drive=2 to hdmi_drive=2
6. Change #config_hdmi_boost=4 to config_hdmi_boost=4
7. Save the file.

Once these changes are done, safely disconnect the microSD card reader from the Windows computer.

3.4.4 Boot up the Pi

Let's boot up the Pi for the first time with the microSD card we prepared. Following are the steps to do the same,

- If you have a HDMI monitor, then connect the monitor directly to the Pi's HDMI port with the HDMI male-male cable. If you have a VGA monitor, use HDMI to VGA adapter to convert HDMI signals to VGA and then connect the monitor to that with VGA-to-VGA cable.

- Insert the microSD card into the microSD card slot of Pi.

- Connect the USB mouse and USB keyboard to the Pi.

- Make sure that the power is switched off at this point. Connect the Pi to the power supply with a micro USB power cable. Connect the monitor to the power supply.

- Check all the connections once and then switch on the power supply of the Pi and the monitor.

At this point, the Pi will start booting up.

For all the models with single core processors, the boot screen show a single image of raspberry fruit in the top left corner. For models with quad core processors, the boot screen show a four images of raspberry fruit in the top left corner.

Once the Pi boots up, following is the screenshot of the Raspbian OS, *(figure 3.23)*

Figure 3.23 Raspbian OS Desktop image

3.5 config.txt and raspi-config

Raspberry Pi does not have the BIOS like desktop computers. BIOS stands for Binary Input Output Statement. BIOS stores the settings for booting up a computer. As the Pi family of computers do not have any BIOS, all the settings are stored in a file known as `config.txt` which resides in the **boot** partition. If you read the microSD card that has Raspbian OS on it, then it will appear as a disk named as boot in a Windows and Mac computers. You will not be able to read other partitions from Windows and Mac computers. If you read the same card with a Linux distribution computer then it will show all the partitions. We have already seen in this chapter how to edit this file for the VGA display. We can tweak other settings too by modifying the `config.txt`. However, this is cumbersome process and Raspbian OS comes with a couple of utilities for the same. The utility that we are going to discuss is `raspi-config` utility that can be launched from the Raspbian OS command line **LXTerminal**. We can find LXTerminal at the top left corner of the Raspbian taskbar. It will be an icon as shown in figure 3.24,

Figure 3.24 Raspbian OS Desktop image

Click the icon and the following window will appear, *(figure 3.25)*

Figure 3.25 LXTerminal window

This is the command line utility of Linux. We can run commands here and interact with the OS directly. Now run the following command here,

```
sudo raspi-config
```

This will invoke the utility and it will look like below as shown in figure 3.26,

```
1 Change User Password  Change password for the
2 Network Options        Configure network settin
3 Boot Options           Configure options for st
4 Localisation Options   Set up language and regi
5 Interfacing Options    Configure connections to
6 Overclock              Configure overclocking f
7 Advanced Options       Configure advanced setti
8 Update                 Update this tool to the
9 About raspi-config     Information about this c



            <Select>                    <Finish>
```

Figure 3.26 raspi-config utility

The very first thing we may want to do is to set the localization options. The most important is the keyboard layout. You may want to change it to American rather than British. Change the other settings like Locale, Timezone, and Wi-Fi country. *(figure 3.27)*

```
I1 Change Locale          Set up language and regi
I2 Change Timezone        Set up timezone to match
I3 Change Keyboard LayouSet the keyboard layout
I4 Change Wi-fi Country Set the legal channels u
```

Figure 3.27 Localization options

We also have to change the **Interfacing Options** and enable **SSH** and **VNC**, *(figure 3.28)*

```
P1 Camera                Enable/Disable connectio
P2 SSH                   Enable/Disable remote co
P3 VNC                   Enable/Disable graphical
P4 SPI                   Enable/Disable automatic
P5 I2C                   Enable/Disable automatic
P6 Serial                Enable/Disable shell and
P7 1-Wire                Enable/Disable one-wire
P8 Remote GPIO           Enable/Disable remote ac
```

Figure 3.28 Interfacing Options

Under the **Advanced Options**, in the **Memory Split**, allocate 16 MB to the GPU. Then, choose **Exapnd Filesystem**. This will allow us to use the storage space on the entire microSD. *(figure 3.29)*

```
A1 Expand Filesystem       Ensures that all of the
A2 Overscan                You may need to configur
A3 Memory Split            Change the amount of mem
A4 Audio                   Force audio out through
A5 Resolution              Set a specific screen re
A6 Pixel Doubling          Enable/Disable 2x2 pixel
A7 GL Driver               Enable/Disable experimen
```

Figure 3.29 Advanced Options

Also, once we enable the internet access (we will see that in the next section), don't forget to update the `raspi-config` utility by choosing the **Update** option from the main menu. Once you choose **Finish** option in the main menu, it will ask you for restart. This will reboot the Pi and boot to desktop again.

3.6 Connect to Network

Now, we will learn how to connect Raspberry Pi to network and internet. We can do it either manually by editing `/etc/network/interfaces` file or through GUI. We will see both the ways.

3.6.1 Connect to WiFi

On the right hand top corner, you can see the Wi-Fi icon where one can discover the Wi-Fi network and connect to it by providing the credentials, *(figure 3.30)*

Figure 3.30 Advanced Options

You can connect to the Wi-Fi manually by editing the `/etc/network/interfaces` file.

Run the following command in the terminal,

```
sudo mv /etc/network/interfaces /etc/network/
interfaces.bkp
```

This will back up the original file where we can restore it from in case something goes wrong.

To edit the file, you can run the following command in the terminal,

```
sudo leafpad /etc/network/interfaces
```

Paste the following lines to the file,

```
source-directory /etc/network/interfaces.d
auto lo
iface lo inet loopback

auto wlan0
allow-hotplug wlan0
iface wlan0 inet dhcp
wpa-ssid "ASHWIN"
wpa-psk "internet"
```

You will have to change the SSID and the key in the above lines as per your own WiFi network. Once done, run the following command,

```
sudo service networking restart
```

This will restart the networking service of the Pi and connect to the WiFi.

3.6.2 Connect to Wired Network

We can connect to a wired network using the Ethernet port. Plug it the network cable there and for static IP address copy the following code in the `/etc/network/interfaces` file.

```
source-directory /etc/network/interfaces.d
auto lo
iface lo inet loopback

auto eth0
```

```
allow-hotplug eth0
iface eth0 inet static

# Your static IP
address 192.168.0.2
# Your gateway IP
gateway 192.168.0.1
netmask 255.255.255.0
# Your network address family
network 192.168.0.0
broadcast 192.168.0.255
```

In case you want to take the advantage of the Dynamic Host Configuration Protocol (DHCP) of your gateway (router/modem) then use the following setting,

```
source-directory /etc/network/interfaces.d
auto lo
iface lo inet loopback
auto eth0
allow-hotplug eth0
iface eth0 inet dhcp
```

Once you have made changes, restart the networking service with the following command,

```
sudo service networking restart
```

This will connect the Pi to the wired network through Ethernet.

3.6.3 Check the Status of Connection

We can check the status of the connection by running the following command,

```
ifconfig
```

This will return the details of the network including the IP address assigned to the Pi.

We can also check the connectivity with the internet by running the following command,

```
ping -c4 www.google.com
```

This will check if www.google.com is reachable from the Pi.

3.7 Remote Connection to Raspberry Pi

We can remotely connect to the Raspberry Pi over the network. We will now learn how to do that within our local network. Make sure you have enabled SSH and VNC for this.

3.7.1 Accessing Command Prompt with PuTTY and Bitwise SSH Client

In case you want to access the command prompt of the Pi then we can use PuTTY SSH client. Download and install PuTTY client from https://www.putty.org/. Once done open the client by searching for PuTTY in the Windows search bar. The client will look as follows, *(figure 3.31)*

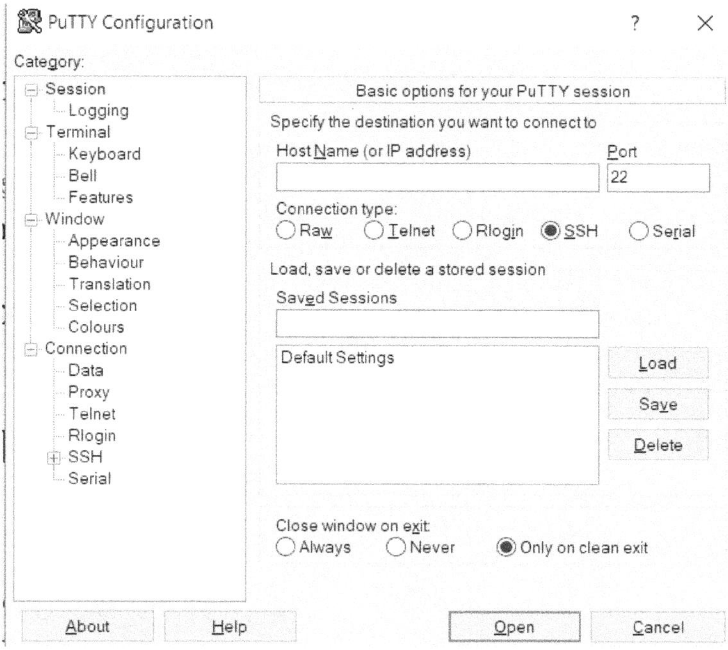

Figure 3.31 PuTTY client

In the above window *(figure 3.31)*, just enter the IP address of the Pi and click **Open** button and you'll be connected to the Pi. It will ask for the username and the password that are **pi** and **raspberry** respectively by default. Once done, it will bring up a window as shown in figure 3.32,

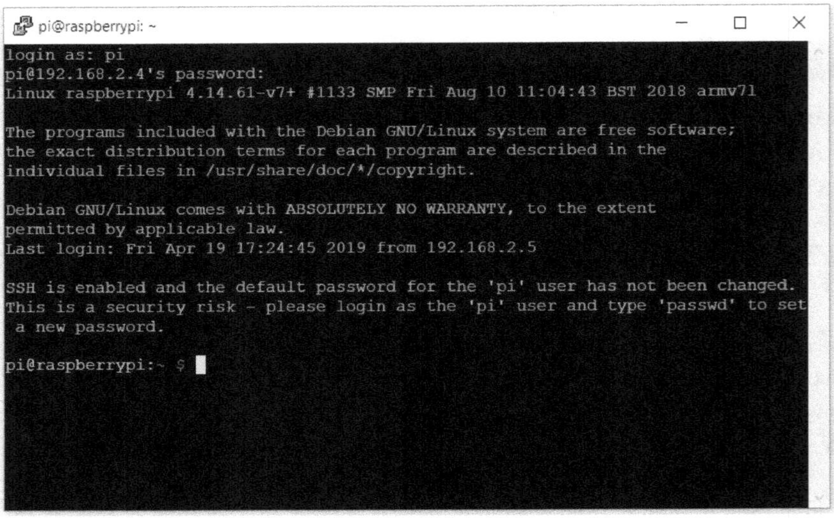

Figure 3.32 PuTTY client

This is the terminal of Raspberry Pi. We can run any command from here that does not involve invoking the GUI. PuTTY client is good enough for the beginners. However, there are more advanced clients available for terminal remote connection. I prefer to use **Bitvise SSH Client**. You can download it from https://www.bitvise.com/ssh-client-download. It comes with the features like facility to save the username/ password combination for repeated usage and FTP file transfer between hosts. Following is the screenshot of the bitwise SSH client in action, *(figure 3.33)*

Figure 3.33 bitwise SSH client

Following is the screenshot of the file transfer window. We can see the Windows filesystem on the left and Raspbian filesystem on the right, *(figure 3.34)*

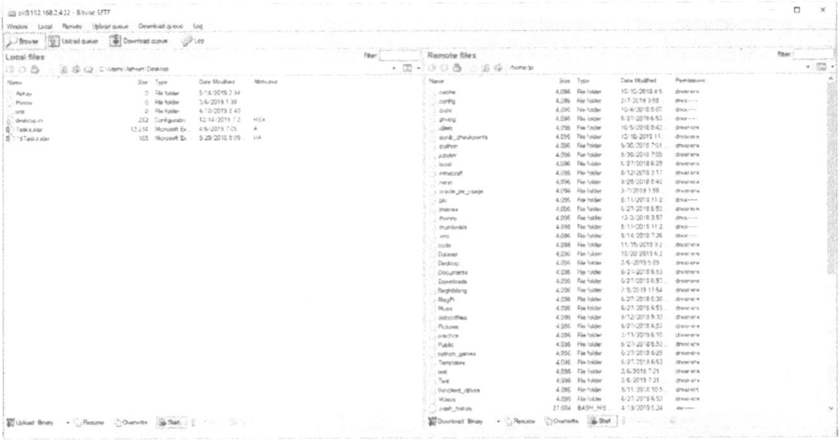

Figure 3.34 Bitwise File Transfer Window

As I have said earlier, I personally prefer to work with bitwise due to added features and ease of usage.

3.7.2 Remote Desktop with RDP and VNC

We have seen a couple of ways to connect to the Pi remotely and access its command prompt and transfer files. However, it is difficult to get GUI applications to work with the SSH. So, we will see a couple of methods for connecting to the desktop remotely.

- **Remote Desktop Protocol**

  We can connect to a Linux remote desktop from Windows using **Remote Desktop Protocol (RDP)**. For that, we first need to install xrdp on Raspberry Pi with the following command,

```
sudo apt-get install xrdp
```

Then, we have to reboot the Pi with the following command,

```
sudo reboot -h now
```

This will restart the Pi. Search for **Remote Desktop Connection** in the Windows search bar. Open the application. Enter all the details like IP address and credentials, *(figure 3.35)*

Figure 3.35 Remote Desktop Connection

Once you click the **Connect** button, you will have to enter the credential to connect to Pi. The remote desktop window will be as follows, *(figure 3.36)*

Figure 3.36 Remote Desktop Window

- VNC

  VNC stands for Virtual Network Computing. It is used to access Linux desktop from other devices. Install VNC server on Pi with the following command,

```
sudo apt-get install realvnc-vnc-server
```

Download and install the VNC viewer for windows from https://www.realvnc.com/en/connect/download/viewer/.

Open the RealVNC viewer and create a new connection from the **File** menu. Following it the window for creating a new connection, *(figure 3.37)*

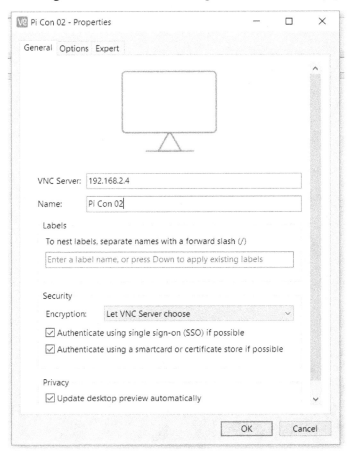

Figure 3.37 New connection window

Once you create a connection, double click it to connect. It will ask you for the credentials as follows, *(figure 3.38)*

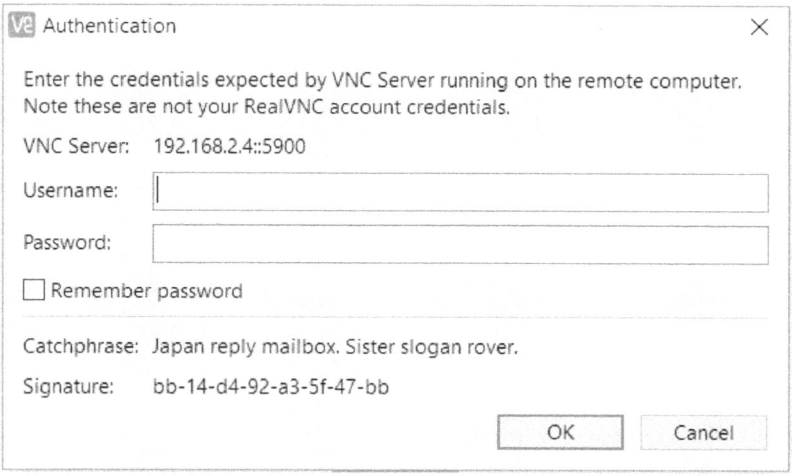

Figure 3.38 New connection window

Following is the screenshot of a RealVNC in the action, *(figure 3.39)*

Figure 3.39 RealVNC in action

3.8 Updating Raspberry Pi

We can update various aspects of software in Raspberry Pi. We can update `raspi-config`, firmware, and Raspbian OS. Let's see how to update them one by one.

We can update `raspi-config` from the main menu **Update** option, *(figure 3.40)*

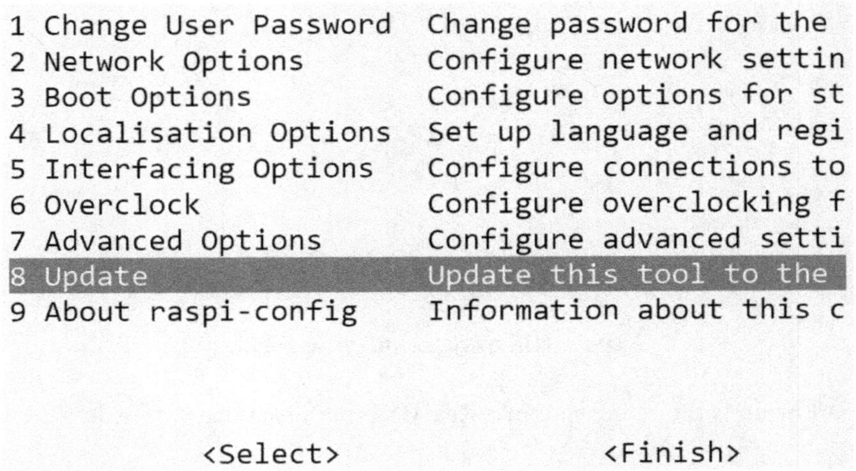

```
1 Change User Password    Change password for the
2 Network Options         Configure network settin
3 Boot Options            Configure options for st
4 Localisation Options    Set up language and regi
5 Interfacing Options     Configure connections to
6 Overclock               Configure overclocking f
7 Advanced Options        Configure advanced setti
8 Update                  Update this tool to the
9 About raspi-config      Information about this c



           <Select>                    <Finish>
```

Figure 3.40 Updating the raspi-config utility

We can update the firmware with the following command,

```
sudo rpi-config
```

We can update the Raspbian OS and packages with the following commands,

```
sudo apt-get update
sudo apt-get dist-upgrade -y
```

3.9 Shutting Down and Restarting Raspberry Pi

We can shut down Raspberry Pi with the following command,

```
sudo shutdown -h now
```

We can reboot Raspberry Pi with the following command,

```
sudo reboot -h now
```

3.10 Why to use Raspberry Pi

Raspberry Pi is the most popular single board computer in the world. It is a low cost and low power consumption computer. If you have a limited budget and you still want to learn programming then Raspberry Pi is the most affordable option available in the market. Also plenty of documentation, books, examples, and help is available online in case the learners face any roadblock.

3.11 Summary

In this chapter, we learned the basics of Single Board Computers and their history. We saw many examples of SBCs. Then we proceeded to learn the most famous SBC of our era, Raspberry Pi, in detail. We learned how to setup Raspberry Pi and how to connect to it remotely. In the next chapter, we will learn Python 3 basics. We will learn how to write a simple "Hello World!" program and execute it on different platforms in different ways. We will also have a look at various Integrated Development Environments (IDEs) for Python 3 programming.

Exercise

To have more and thorough understanding of Raspberry Pi and Raspbian OS, complete the following exercise,

- Explore all the utilities in Raspbian OS
- I have not covered all the options in `raspi-config` utility. Explore rest of the options.
- Visit and explore all the URLs provided in the chapter.

CHAPTER 4
Python 3 Basics

In the last chapter, we saw what single board computers are. We also explored Raspberry Pi family of single board computers in detail and learned how to setup Raspberry Pi. We saw the installation procedure for Raspbian OS on Pi in detail and then how to connect to Raspberry Pi remotely.

In this chapter, we will cover the basics of Python in great detail. We will study history and origin of Python programming language.

4.1 History of Python Programming Language

The Python programming language was born in the late 1980s. Its implementation was started in December 1989 by Guido van Rossum who was working at National Research Institute for Mathematics and Computer Science (CWI) in the Netherlands. It is developed as a successor to ABC programming language. ABC itself was inspired by SETL, a high-level programming language. Python was envisioned to be capable of exception handling and interfacing with the Amoeba operating system. Python was named after the famous BBC TV comedy show **Monty Python's Flying Circus**.

Van Rossum is Python's principal author and was given title by the Python community, **Benevolent Dictator for Life (BDFL)**. He stepped down as a leader of Python Community on 12 July 2018.

In February 1991, Guido van Rossum published the code labeled as version 0.9.0 of Python to alt.sources. The features present in this release were classes with inheritance, exception handling, functions, and the core datatypes of list, dict, str, and so on.

Python 2.0 was released on October 16, 2000, with many major new features like:

- a cycle-detecting garbage collector for memory management

- reference counting
- support for Unicode

4.2 Why Python 3

Python 3.0, is a major, backwards-incompatible version. It was initially released on 3 December 2008. It is not guaranteed that Python 2.x code will be interpreted and executed as it is by Python 3.x without any errors. Many of major features of Python 3.x have also been back ported to the backwards-compatible Python 2.6 and 2.7.

The final 2.x version 2.7 release came out in mid-2010. Python 2.7's end-of-life date was initially set at ٢٠١٥. However it was then postponed to 2020 out of concern that a lot of existing production code and third party libraries could not easily be forward-ported to Python 3 in time. You can read about it on PEP 37 page at https://www.python.org/dev/peps/pep-0373/. If you are reading this book in 2020 or after then Python 2 is not supported anymore officially. If you are reading this book before 2020 then you can visit https://pythonclock.org to know how many days are left for Python 2 official support to end. Python's wiki page https://wiki.python.org/moin/Python2orPython3 says,

Python 2.x is legacy, Python 3.x is the present and future of the language.

We can additionally visit https://python3statement.org/ to see what projects will be supporting Python 3 only post 1 January 2020. Other third-party organizations **may** provide support to the projects listed in the webpage mentioned above for Python 2 on paid basis. Many third party projects have already made transition and have stopped supporting any Python 2.x.

If the organization you are working for still has a significant codebase written in Python 2 then **now** is the best time to start migrating all the code to Python 3 in steps. There are many tools and utilities available to migrate your Python 2 code to Python 3. Discussion of these utilities is beyond the scope of this book.

4.3 Features and Benefits of Python Programming Language

Python is a widely used programming language. The following are the features and benefits of Python programming language.

- **Easy to learn and read**

The code written in Python follows the rules of indentation and it is very easy to learn python programming. Because of this, this generation of programmers is learning programming with Python as their first programming language.

- **Cross-platform language and portable**

  Python interpreter is available for all the major OS platforms including Windows, UNIX, Linux, Android, and Mac. Also, the program written on one platform are mostly portable except platform specific functionality.

- **Free and Open Source**

  Python is free to use and its code is open source. That's why there are many interpreters available for Python.

- **Object oriented**

  Python is an object-oriented programming language. It comes with a lot of modern object-oriented features like modules, classes, objects, and exception handling.

- **Large standard library**

  As a part of batteries-included philosophy of Python, it comes with a very large standard library which helps programmers with various routine programming related tasks.

- **Plenty of third-party libraries**

  Python also boasts, plenty of third-party developed libraries. Python Package Index is the repository of all these libraries supported by Python that can be conveniently downloaded and installed.

- **GUI programming language**

  Python has many libraries for GUI programming. Examples of GUI libraries are Kivy, PyQT, Tkinter, PyGUI, WxPython, and PySide.

- **Interpreted**

  Python programming language is interpreted which makes it easy for programmers to debug and learn programming.

- **Extensible**

  Python is easily extended with C/C++/Java. In large programming projects, it is quite common to see important or critical code written in C or C++ and interfaced with Python.

- **Dynamically typed**

  In dynamically typed languages, names are bound to object at the time of execution. Python follows that, thus it is dynamically types programming language. In Python, we can assign any value to a variable and we do not have to declare the type of the variables.

- **Interactive mode**

  Python has interpreter / interactive mode which is very useful for beginners and debugging. There are many third-party tools like Jupyter that allow us to program interactively in the web browser. This makes collaboration easy.

4.4 IDLE and Hello World!

Integrated Development and Learning Environment (IDLE) is the IDE that comes with the Python interpreter provided by Python Software Foundation that we learned to install on Windows. In this section, we will understand to use this IDE and learn how to write and execute customary "Hello World!" program.

Go to the search bar of Windows and search for IDLE or Python and it will show IDLE program, *(figure 4.1)*

Figure 4.1 Starting IDLE

This will launch Python Shell **(Interpreter)** as follows, *(figure 4.2)*

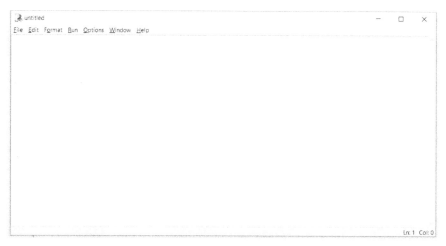

Figure 4.2 Python IDLE Shell/Interpreter

We will see it later how to use this interpreter. Click **File** and then **New File**. This will open the editor for writing and executing Python program, *(figure 4.3)*

Figure 4.3 Python IDLE Code Editor

Type the following code in the editor and save it in the disk,

```
print("Hello World!")
```

The editor will look as follows, *(figure 4.4)*

Figure 4.4 Hello World!

Now, if you Click **Run** and then **Run Module** or directly press **F5** key on the keyboard, it will execute the program and will show the output of the execution of the program in the Python Shell or Interpreter. Following is the output, *(figure 4.5)*

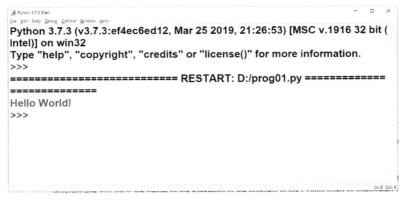

Figure 4.5 Hello World! Output in the shell

This is how we can write and run a Python program in Windows.

We can run the program from command prompt. Open Windows command prompt and run the python program with the following command,

```
python prog01.py
```

If the program `prog01.py` is not in the same directory where we're running the program then we need to provide absolute path of the program. Once we run this command, the program will be run by the Python 3 interpreter. The output is as follows, *(figure 4.6)*

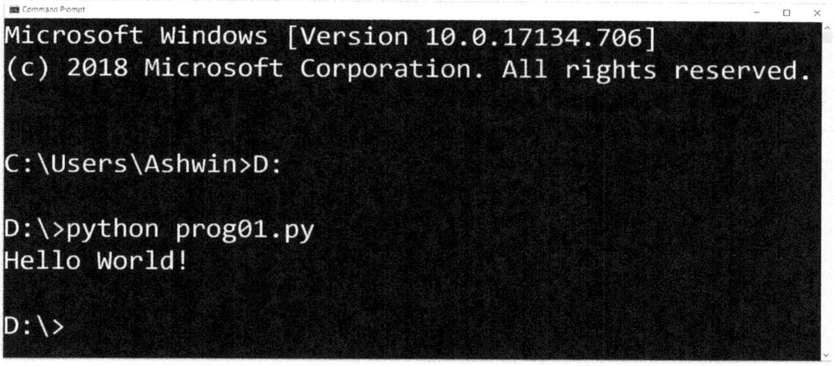

Figure 4.6 Output of Python program in Windows Command prompt

It is not mandatory to use IDLE to write Python program. We can even use a simpler text editor like **Notepad** or **Wordpad**.

4.5 Python Interpreter Mode

Earlier, we saw how to write a Python program and run that with interpreter. That was known as **script mode** where we keep ready the entire program ready beforehand and then feed it to the interpreter to execute all the statements one by one to see the output.

There is another way to execute the Python statements. It is known as **interpreter mode**. We can invoke interpreter of Python by typing in python on command prompt or by opening IDLE. In the interpreter mode, we have to input the statements one by one and the statement or code block is executed one at a time much like command prompt commands. This allows beginners to debug their programs easily and learn Python programming faster. Open the Python 3 interpreter on command prompt and IDLE and practice by running following two statements,

```
>>> print("Hello World!")
Hello World!
>>> 1 + 1
2
```

Unless we are using Jupyter notebook, it is not possible to save, reopen, and execute all the statements. We will see Jupyter notebook in detail in the next chapter.

4.6 Python on Raspberry Pi Raspbian OS

Raspbian OS is a variant of Debian Linux distribution tailored for Raspberry Pi. Almost all the latest Linux distributions have both interpreters, Python 2 and Python 3, installed by default. Running the command `python` in the terminal invokes Python 2 interpreter and running the command `python3` in the terminal invokes Python 3 interpreter. We can invoke IDLE in two ways. First way is to run the command `idle3` in the terminal. You can find the terminal program in the Raspbian taskbar, *(figure 4.7)*

Figure 4.7 Terminal Icon in the taskbar

The other way is to open it from **Programming** in the Raspbian Menu as follows, *(figure 4.8)*

Figure 4.8 Python 3 IDLE in Programming section

Create and run a "Hello World!" program using IDLE. To run the program from the terminal, run the following command,

```
python3 prog01.py
```

There is one more way of running the Python programs from terminal. Create a Python code file with the following code,

```
#!/usr/bin/python3
print("Hello World!")
```

The first line in the code above tells us the path of the Python 3 interpreter in Raspbian OS. #! is known as **shebang**. It is used to convey the path of interpreter to shell that is running the script. Once you save the program, change the permissions using the following command in the terminal,

```
chmod 755 prog01.py
```

This will change the permissions of the file to executable by the owner. Now, we can directly run the program by executing the following command on the terminal,

```
./prog01.py
```

The output will be shown on the command prompt. This is how we can run the Python programs on the command prompt of Linux.

4.7 Other editors in the Raspbian

The Raspbian OS has **Geany** and **Thonny** code editors are pre-installed on Raspbian OS and you can run your Python 3 programs on these. You can find both the editors in the **Programming** sections of Raspbian menu. **Geany** is a popular editor that can run Python 2 and Python 3 programs. In Geany editor, in the menubar, under the **Build** menu, in the **Set Build Commands** menu option, we can set the interpreter to run our programs as follows, *(figure 4.9)*

Figure 4.9 Setting the interpreter in Geany

In the figure above (figure 4.9), the text box highlighted with red square is used to set the Python interpreter for your program. For running Python 3 programs, make sure that it has value **python3 "%f"** as shown above (figure.4.9)

Also, in the **Thonny** editor, under **Tools** in the menu, in the **Options**, we can change the interpreter with the dropdown in the **interpreter** tab as shown in the screenshot below, *(figure 4.10)*

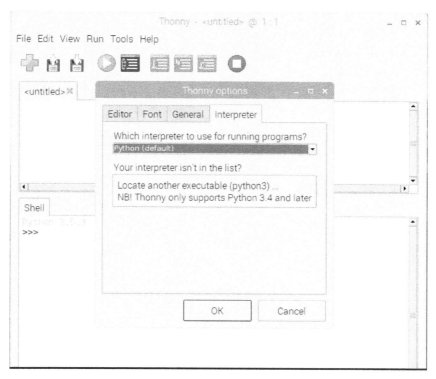

Figure 4.10 Setting the interpreter in Thonny

Also, there are a few non-IDE code editor like **leafpad** and **vi** in Raspbian that can be used for writing Python programs.

4.8 Summary

In this chapter, we learned the history of Python and why to move forward with Python 3. We also saw how to write simple Python 3 program and to run it on the different platforms. In the next chapter, we will explore Scientific Python Ecosystem, pip, and Jupyter notebook for Python programming.

Exercise

As an exercise to this chapter, explore the all the URLs mentioned in the chapter.

## CHAPTER 5

Introduction to the Scientific Python Ecosystem

In the last chapter, we learned the history and basics of Python 3. We also ran our very first Python program on a Windows computer and a Raspberry Pi Raspbian OS.

In this chapter, we will study the basics of Scientific Python Ecosystem. We will see PyPI and pip in detail and learn how to program interactively with Jupyter notebook and IPython.

5.1 Python Package Index (PyPI) and pip

Python comes with a vast library that take care of lot of programming needs. However, many advanced features and data structures are not available with Python's built in library and there are many third-party library projects for that. Many of these projects are available at **Python Package Index (PyPI)**. You can visit PyPI at https://pypi.org/. Its homepage says,

The Python Package Index (PyPI) is a repository of software for the Python programming language.

We can install the packages and software libraries for Python hosted at PyPI with command-line utility known as **pip**. pip stands for "*pip install packages*" or "*pip installs python*". It is a recursive acronym that includes itself when expanded. For Python 3, we have pip3 command. We can run it on Windows or Raspberry Pi. It comes with all the distributions of Python 3. So, we do not have to install it separately.

To see the list of packages installed on the current Python 3 environment, use the following command,

```
pip3 list
```

To search for a specific package in the PyPI, use the following command,

```
pip3 search numpy
```

To install a specific package from the PyPI, use the following command,

```
pip3 install numpy
```

To uninstall a specific package from your computer, use the following command,

```
pip3 uninstall numpy
```

In case, you run into permission issues while running the commands on Raspberry Pi, the commands must be preceded with `sudo`.

5.2 Scientific Python Ecosystem

Scientific Python Ecosystem is dominated by **SciPy** and related projects. Let's have a detailed look at SciPy first.

SciPy stands for **Scientific Python**. It is a Python-based ecosystem of open-source software for mathematics, science, and engineering. You can read about it in more detail at https://www.scipy.org/. SciPy has many distinct yet related and collaboratively developed libraries. Following are the core libraries,

- **NumPy**

    NumPy is the fundamental package for scientific computing with Python. Nearly all the other libraries in the Scientific Python Ecosystem use ndarray data structure from NumPy. We will see NumPy in detail in the subsequent chapters. Visit http://www.numpy.org/ for more information.

- **SciPy library**

    The SciPy library is one of the core packages that make up the SciPy stack. It provides many user-friendly and efficient numerical routines such as routines for numerical integration and optimization. You can find more information about it on https://www.scipy.org/scipylib/index.html.

- **Matplotlib**

    It is a 2D plotting library in Python and creates publication quality visualizations. It can create 2D and 3D visualizations of the scientific data. Find out more about it on https://matplotlib.org/. We have a chapter dedicated for matplotlib.

- **SymPy**

  It is a library for symbolic computations. Visit https://www.sympy.org/en/index.html for more information.

- **Pandas**

  Pandas is an open source, BSD-licensed library providing high-performance, easy-to-use data structures and data analysis tools. You can find more information about Pandas at. http://pandas.pydata.org/. Pandas is mostly used for data science and visualization.

- **IPython**

  IPython provides environment for interactive computing for Python. We will discuss IPython in detail in this chapter. Please check http://ipython.org/ for more information.

5.3 IPython and Jupyter

IPython is an interactive computing tool for Python. You can run it in the command prompt as well as in a browser. IPython supports Python language only. However, many of its features like notebook and notebook server are so appealing that IPython evolved into another related project known as **Jupyter**. Jupyter supports many other programming languages. The kernel for Python is still provided by IPython in the Jupyter project. We can find more information about Jupyter project at https://jupyter.org/. In this book, we will use Jupyter extensively for all the programming examples. Run the following command at the Windows command prompt,

```
pip3 install jupyter
```

It will install Jupyter on Windows computer.

To install Jupyter on Raspberry Pi, run the following commands one after another in the terminal,

```
sudo pip3 uninstall ipykernel
sudo pip3 install ipykernel==4.8.0
sudo pip3 install jupyter
sudo pip3 install prompt-toolkit==2.0.5
```

This will install and the correct version of all the dependencies on Raspberry Pi.

Once you install Jupyter notebook, it can be launched by running the following command on Windows command prompt or Raspberry Pi terminal,

```
jupyter notebook
```

When we run Jupyter notebook, it starts a notebook server in the command prompt and launches an instance of Jupyter notebook on the default web browser of your computer as follows, *(figure 5.1)*

Figure 5.1 Jupyter instance

The screenshot shown in *figure 5.1*, gives us an instance of Jupyter. We can see the files and the folders in the directory where we launched the Jupyter from in the command prompt. It treats the directory where we launched it from in the command prompt as the root directory for the current instance.

Also on the command prompt, it will show the execution log of the Jupyter. You can find the following string in that log,

```
Copy/paste this URL into your browser when you
connect for the first time,
    to login with a token:
                                        http://
localhost:8888/?token=e7f8818e7673d0d4dbd46
f7376e8b4bb1a07aebc91e6a64c
```

In the log above, you can find the URL that contains the token for the current session. In case you want to use some other browser for Jupyter notebook then you can directly use the URL.

You can also search for http://localhost:8888/ in the address bar of the browser. In this case it asks for a token. Just copy and paste the token from the execution log (the string after `token=` in the above log) and click Log In button, *(figure 5.2)*

Figure 5.2 Jupyter login through token

This will start an instance of Jupyter, just like earlier instance.

This way, we can launch an instance of Jupyter. Now, let's see how to use it for Python 3 programming. Click the **New** button in the top right corner. It will show us a drop-down with a list of various programming languages installed on your Windows computer or Raspberry Pi. It detects the Python interpreter by referring the PATH variable in your system. *(figure 5.3)*

Figure 5.3 New Python 3 Notebook

It will launch a Jupyter notebook for Python. By default it will be untitled. Also, a corresponding file **Untitled.ipynb** will be created in the current directory where we launched the Jupyter notebook in the command prompt. There is also option to create a new directory and a text file. If you want to consolidate your notebooks in a single directory, you might want to create a new directory and create the notebook there. Following is a screenshot of a notebook, *(figure 5.4)*

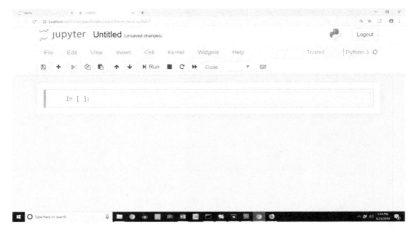

Figure 5.4 Untitled notebook

You can double click the name of the notebook (in this case **Untitled**), a popup will appear where you can add a new name, *(figure 5.5)*

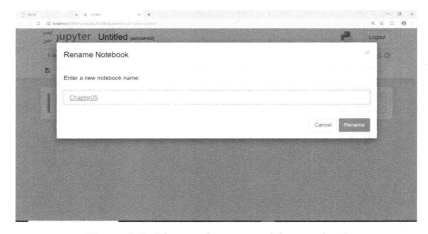

Figure 5.5 Change the name of the notebook

Once we click the **Rename** button, it will change the name of the notebook and corresponding ipynb file in the filesystem. For this book, I am creating one notebook for every chapter and all these notebooks will be available with the book CD. In case you want to use any of them, just copy them into a directory of your computer or Pi and launch the Jupyter notebook from that directory from the command prompt on Windows or terminal on Pi. Once launched, all the ipynb files you copied will be shown in the Jupyter notebook as a list.

Let's start using the notebook. We will have a look at all the important feature that we are going to use in the book. I frequently use all the features that I am about to explain and I believe that these are the most important features of the Jupyter notebook that any beginner will find quite useful. In the toolbor, if you click the dropdown, it will show four options. The first is **Code** and second is **Markdown**. *(figure 5.6)*

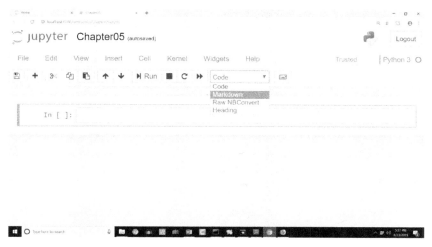

Figure 5.6 Toolbar Dropdown Options

Jupyter notebook can have different types of cells. For example, we might want to have a cell for a code and another for heading explaining use of the code segment. For headings, we use **Rich Text Format**. It is implemented with Markdown which is a **lightweight markup language** with plain text formatting syntax. When you choose Markdown from the toolbar, it converts the current cell into a Markdown cell where we can add some rich text with markdown now. After choosing markdown from the toolbar, just add the following code to the current cell,

```
# Hello World! Program
```

Then, click the run button in the toolbar. The Jupyter notebook will interpret current statement as a markdown and reader it in the H1 style heading as follows, *(figure 5.7)*

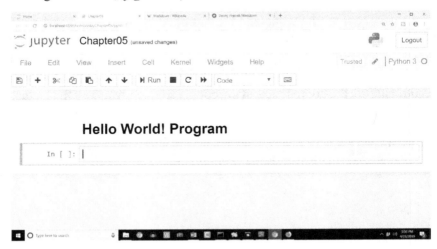

Figure 5.7 H1 Heading with Markdown

This way, we can introduce the cells with rich text contents in our Jupyter notebook. The markdown syntax is out of scope for the book as we will be using it for headings and sub-headings only. In case you want to use other features of markdown, just check https://en.wikipedia.org/wiki/Markdown and https://daringfireball.net/projects/markdown/.

Once we execute the current cell contents with the **Run** button, apart from rendering the output, Jupyter notebook creates a new cell and sets the cursor there. By default, all the new cells will be of type **Code**. Now, in the new cell type in the following Python 3 code,

```
print("Hello World!")
```

And then run the cell. It will interpret it as Python statement and show the output like below, *(figure 5.8)*

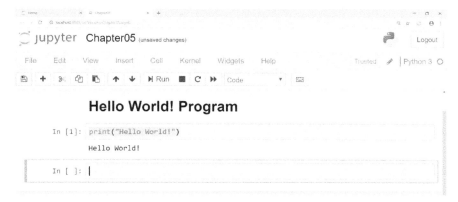

Figure 5.8 Output of a Python 3 code snippet

This way, the Jupyter notebook can have cells of markdown and code type and this allows us to have multiple types of output along with the code to be part of the same notebook. Another important feature of the Jupyter notebook is that, we can re-edit the already executed cells and execute the re-edited code again. This allows us to edit the code cells as per our requirement.

Let's have a look at the other options on the toolbar. On the extreme left, we have the save button. The button adjacent to it (which has + sign) will create a new cell immediately after the currently highlighted cell and set the cursor there. This feature is useful if you want to add a new cell in between existing cell. After that, we have group of buttons for cut, copy, and paste operations. After that we have a group of two buttons (up and down arrow). These are to shift the positions of current cell up and down. Finally, we have a group of four buttons related to the execution of cells. First button is Run, second button (filled in square) is for interrupting the kernel that results in interrupting in the execution of cell if execution is underway, third button is for restarting kernel, and fourth option is for restarting the kernel with re-run of the whole notebook.

Also, let's have look at the most used option in the Menubar which is above the toolbar. Most of the menu options are similar to the options present in any other text or code editor. I will discuss the menu option that is used to clear the output of execution of entire notebook at once. In **Cell**, under **All Outputs**, click **Clear**. This will clear the output of execution of the entire notebook, *(figure 5.9)*

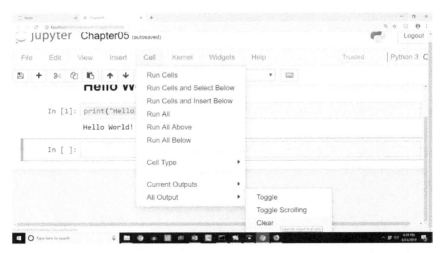

Figure 5.9 Clearing the output of execution of the entire notebook

This way, we can use the Jupyter notebook for Python programming. We can also show visualizations in the notebook itself. We will see that in the next chapter.

5.4 Summary

In this chapter, we had a brief introduction to Scientific Python Ecosystem. We also learned PyPI and pip for Python. We then saw how we can create interactive notebooks with Jupyter notebook program. Thus, Jupyter is an important tool for collaboration. People can explain their ideas to group of people in the real-time with code examples and then share the Jupyter notebook that contains code, rich text, and visualizations with the participants. Thus, Jupyter notebook is a very useful tool in the academic institutions, research organizations, and technology based organizations where Python 3 programming is used for scientific computing.

In the next chapter, we will see NumPy in detail and will also have a very brief introduction to the matplotlib library.

Exercise

As an exercise to this chapter, explore all the URLs presented in this chapter. Also explore the remaining options in the menu bar in the Jupyter notebook.

CHAPTER 6
Introduction to NumPy and Matplotlib

In the last chapter, we learned introduction to pip utility and Python Package Index. We also had a brief introduction to the Scientific Python Ecosystem and core members of it. We studied Jupyter notebook too for Python programming. In this chapter, we will study NumPy in detail. The basics of ndarray data structure in NumPy. Also, we will see NumPy routines to create and modify NumPy ndarrays. We will get introduced to a plotting library, matplotlib and see a few code examples of it.

6.1 Introduction to NumPy

NumPy's website www.numpy.org says that,

NumPy is the fundamental package for scientific computing with Python.

The following are the benefits of NumPy,

- a powerful N-dimensional array object known as ndarray
- sophisticated ndarray creation and manipulation functions
- useful linear algebra, Fourier transform, and random number functions

6.1.1 Ndarray

Ndarray (or N-d array) is a multidimensional data structure in NumPy. Actually, it is the most important data structure in Scientific Python because all other libraries and data structures in Scientific Python stack use NumPy ndarrays in some form or the other to represent data.

All the items in ndarray have same size and type. Just like the other containers in Python, ndarray can be accessed by indexing and can also be sliced. We will see all these operations in detail in this chapter.

6.1.2 Installation of NumPy and Matplotlib

Let's see how to install NumPy and matplotlib on Windows and Raspberry Pi Raspbian OS. We will see matplotlib in detail down the line.

To install the both on Windows, run the following commands in the command prompt,

```
pip3 install numpy
pip3 install matplotlib
```

NumPy comes with Raspbian OS. We just need to update it with the following command in the terminal,

```
sudo pip3 install --upgrade numpy
```

We need to install matplotlib as it does not come with the Raspbian OS.

```
sudo pip3 install matplotlib
```

In order to install NumPy on Linux in general, use the following command in terminal,

```
sudo pip3 install numpy
```

6.2 Getting Started with NumPy Programming

We will start writing code snippets with NumPy now. And, as I mentioned earlier, we will use Jupyter notebook for writing the code snippets. Open the command prompt and run the Jupyter with the following command,

```
jupyter notebook
```

Save the notebook with a filename of your choice. Type in and run the following statement to import NumPy library for the current sessions of the notebook,

```
import numpy as np
```

The following statements creates a one-dimensional ndarray,

```
x = np.array([1, 2, 3], np.int16)
```

In the code above, the function call creates ndarray with the passed arguments. The first argument is a list which has the data and the second argument is the data type of the individual elements of the ndarray. NumPy has quite a lot of data types. The following is the list of them,

np.bool	np.int_	np.longdouble	np.int64	np.float32
np.byte	np.uint	np.csingle	np.uint8	np.float64
np.ubyte	np.longlong	np.cdouble	np.uint16	np.complex64
np.short	np.ulonglong	np.clongdouble	np.uint32	np.complex128
np.ushort	np.half	np.int8	np.uint64	np.float_
np.intc	np.single	np.int16	np.intp	np.complex_
np.uintc	np.double	np.int32	np.uintp	np.float16

We can find out more information about the datatypes at https://www.numpy.org/devdocs/user/basics.types.html.

Run the following statements,

```
print(x)
print(type(x))
```

The first statement will print the ndarray. Second statement will print the type of the object. Following is the output,

```
[1 2 3]
<class 'numpy.ndarray'>
```

Ndarrays follow C style indexing where the first element is stored at position 0 and nth element is stored at position n-1. We can access individual members of the ndarray like below,

```
print(x[0])
```

```
print(x[1])
```

```
print(x[2])
```

The following statement prints the last element in the ndarray,

```
print(x[-1])
```

However, when the index exceeds n-1 then Python interpreter throws error,

```
print(x[3])
```

The above statements raise the following exception,

```
IndexError: index 3 is out of bounds for axis 0 with size 3
```

We can also create a two-dimensional ndarray as follows,

```
x = np.array([[1, 2, 3], [4, 5, 6]], np.int16)
print(x)
```

This will create a two-dimensional array as follows,

```
[[1 2 3]
 [4 5 6]]
```

We can access individual elements of the ndarray as follows,

```
print(x[0, 0])
print(x[0, 1])
print(x[0, 2])
```

We can access entire columns by slicing the ndarray as follows,

```
print(x[:, 0])
print(x[:, 1])
print(x[:, 2])
```

Following are the respective outputs of the statements above,

```
[1 4]
[2 5]
[3 6]
```

We can access entire rows by slicing the ndarray as follows,

```
print(x[0, :])
print(x[1, :])
```

Following are the respective outputs of the statements,

```
[1 2 3]
[4 5 6]
```

Similarly, we can create a three-dimensional ndarray as follows,

```
x = np.array([[[1, 2, 3], [4, 5, 6]], [[0, -1, -2],
[-3, -4, -5]]], np.int16)
print(x)
```

We can access individual members of three-dimensional arrays as follows,

```
print(x [0, 0, 0])
print(x [1, 1, 2])
```

We can slice the three-dimensional arrays as follows,

```
print(x[:, 1, 1])
print(x[:, :, 1])
```

6.3 Ndarray Properties

Let's understand the properties of ndarray. For that, we will create a three-dimensional array as follows,

```
x = np.array([[[1, 2, 3], [4, 5, 6]],[[0, -1, -2],
[-3, -4, -5]]], np.int16)
print(x)
```

It creates the following three-dimensional array,

```
[[[ 1  2  3]
 [ 4  5  6]]

 [[ 0 -1 -2]
 [-3 -4 -5]]]
```

The following code prints the properties of NumPy ndarrays,

```
print(x.shape)
print(x.ndim)
print(x.dtype)
print(x.size)
print(x.nbytes)
```

The output is as follows,

```
(2, 2, 3)
3
int16
12
24
```

The `shape` property returns the shape of the ndarray. `ndim` returns the dimensions of the array. `dtype` refers to the data type of the individual members of the ndarray (and not the data type of the darray object itself). `size` property returns the number of elements in the ndarray. And `nbytes` returns the size of the ndarray in the bytes in the memory. We can also compute the transpose of the ndarray with the following property,

```
print(x.T)
```

6.4 Ndarray Constants

We can represent a few important abstract constants like positive and negative zero and infinity and NAN (not a number) as follows,

```
print(np.inf)
print(np.NAN)
print(np.NINF)
print(np.NZERO)
print(np.PZERO)
```

The following constants are the important scientific constants,

```
print(np.e)
print(np.euler_gamma)
print(np.pi)
```

We can visit the following URL for the complete list of such constants,

https://docs.scipy.org/doc/numpy/reference/constants.html

6.5 Ndarray Creation Routines

Let's learn a few ndarray creation routines. The first function is `empty()` that creates an empty ndarray.

```
x = np.empty([3, 3], np.uint8)
```

The code above creates an empty ndarray. While creating, it is not assigned any values. So, it will have random values assigned to elements.

We can create diagonal matrices of various sizes using `eye()` function,

```
y = np.eye(5, dtype=np.uint8)
print(y)
```

Following is the output,

```
[[1 0 0 0 0]
 [0 1 0 0 0]
 [0 0 1 0 0]
 [0 0 0 1 0]
 [0 0 0 0 1]]
```

We can also change the position of the diagonal as follows,

```
y = np.eye(5, dtype=np.uint8, k=1)
```

```
print(y)
```

Following is the output,

```
[[0 1 0 0 0]
 [0 0 1 0 0]
 [0 0 0 1 0]
 [0 0 0 0 1]
 [0 0 0 0 0]]
```

Another example is,

```
y = np.eye(5, dtype=np.uint8, k=-1)
print(y)
```

We can create an identity matrix as follows,

```
x = np.identity(5, dtype= np.uint8)
print(x)
```

We can create ndarrays where all the elements are 1 as follows,

```
x = np.ones((2, 5, 5), dtype=np.int16)
print(x)
```

Similarly, we can create ndarray where all the elements are zero as follows,

```
x = np.zeros((2, 5, 5, 2), dtype=np.int16)
print(x)
```

We can create ndarray and populate all its elements with a single value,

```
x = np.full((3, 3, 3), dtype=np.int16, fill_value = 5)
print(x)
```

Let's see how we can create triangular matrices with `tri()` function,

```
x = np.tri(3, 3, k=0, dtype=np.uint16)
print(x)
```

The output is as follows,

```
[[1 0 0]
 [1 1 0]
 [1 1 1]]
```

Other examples are,

```
x = np.tri(5, 5, k=1, dtype=np.uint16)
```

```
print(x)
x = np.tri(5, 5, k=-1, dtype=np.uint16)
print(x)
```

Run the above code and see the output for yourself.

We can explicitly create lower triangular matrix as follows,

```
x = np.ones((5, 5), dtype=np.uint8)
y = np.tril(x, k=-1)
print(y)
```

The output is as follows,

```
[[0 0 0 0 0]
 [1 0 0 0 0]
 [1 1 0 0 0]
 [1 1 1 0 0]
 [1 1 1 1 0]]
```

The code for upper triangular matrix is as follows,

```
x = np.ones((5, 5), dtype=np.uint8)
y = np.triu(x, k=0)
```

```
print(y)
```

```
[[1 1 1 1 1]
 [0 1 1 1 1]
 [0 0 1 1 1]
 [0 0 0 1 1]
 [0 0 0 0 1]]
```

Other examples are:

```
x = np.ones((5, 5), dtype=np.uint8)
y = np.triu(x, k=-1)
print(y)
x = np.ones((5, 5), dtype=np.uint8)
y = np.triu(x, k=1)
print(y)
```

6.6 Ndarray Creation Routines with Matplotlib

We know that matplotlib is the plotting and visualization library of Python Scientific ecosystem. Matplotlib supports NumPy ndarrays and accept them as arguments for its plotting routines. Let's have a look at few more NumPy ndarray creation routines and matplotlib plotting routines too. Import the `pyplot` module in matplotlib with the following command,

```
import matplotlib.pyplot as plt
```

`arange()` function creates a series of numbers. Its use is as follows,

```
x = np.arange(5)
print(x)
y=x
```

It creates two ndarrays. Following is the output of the program,

```
[0 1 2 3 4]
```

We can plot both the ndarrays with `plot()` function in `pyplot`. However, before we call the `plot()` function to visualize the ndarrays, we need to enable the Jupyter notebook instance to allow matplotlib visualization. It can be done by executing the following magic command in the Jupyter notebook,

```
%matplotlib inline
```

This will enable matplotlib visualization. Run the following code to visualize the ndarrays,

```
plt.plot(x, y, 'o--')
plt.plot(x, -y, 'o-')
plt.show()
```

The first argument to the `plot()` function call is the list of values for X-axis, the second argument is the list of values for Y-axis, and the third argument is the visualization style. It will automatically create the following output and show it after the current cell in the Jupyter notebook, *(figure 6.1)*

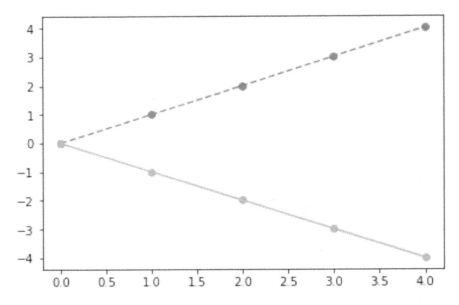

Figure 6.1 Simple plots with matplotlib

We can use `title()` function to add title to the visualization. Run the following code and see the output,

```
plt.plot(x, y, 'o--')
plt.plot(x, -y, 'o-')
plt.title('y=x and y=-x')
plt.show()
```

Similar to `range()`, we have `linspace()` that takes upper limit, lower limit, and number of points for an ndarray as follows,

```
N = 11
x = np.linspace(0, 10, N)
print(x)
y = x
```

The output is as follows,

[0. 1. 2. 3. 4. 5. 6. 7. 8. 9. 10.]

We want to visualize this. Also, we want to turn the axes off,

```
plt.plot(x, y, 'o--')
```

```
plt.axis('off')
```

```
plt.show()
```

The output will be a simple line without any axis as follows, *(figure 6.2)*

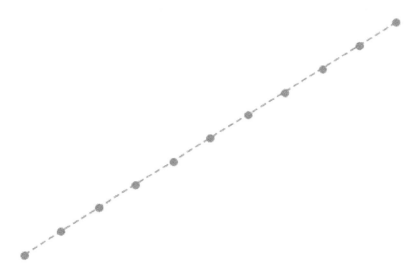

Figure 6.2 `linspace()` *visualized*

We can generate logarithmic data with the `logspace()` as follows,

```
y = np.logspace(0.1, 1, N)
print(y)
plt.plot(x, y, 'o--')
plt.show()
```

The output is as follows, *(figure 6.3)*

```
[ 1.25892541  1.54881662  1.90546072  2.34422882  2.8840315   3.54813389
  4.36515832  5.37031796  6.60693448  8.12830516 10.          ]
```

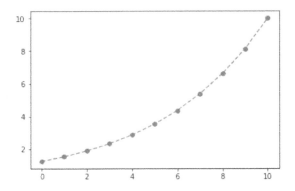

Figure 6.3 `logspace()` *visualized*

We can create a ndarray in geometric progression as follows,

```
y = np.geomspace(0.1, 1000, N)

print(y)

plt.plot(x, y, 'o--')

plt.show()
```

The output is as follows, *(figure 6.4)*

```
[1.00000000e-01 2.51188643e-01 6.30957344e-01 1.58489319e+00
 3.98107171e+00 1.00000000e+01 2.51188643e+01 6.30957344e+01
 1.58489319e+02 3.98107171e+02 1.00000000e+03]
```

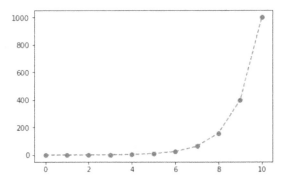

Figure 6.4 `geomspace()` *visualized*

6.7 Random Data Generation

We can generate ndarrays with the random values with a few random functions. Let's see a few examples of these. Have a look at the following code,

```
x = np.random.randint( low = 0, high = 9, size =
10)
print(x)
```

`randint()` generates an ndarray of random numbers with given limits and size as follows,

```
[4 5 3 6 7 6 0 2 3 0]
```

We can also use rand() to create ndarray with given size and dimensions. Following are the examples,

```
x = np.random.rand(3, 3)

print(x)

x = np.random.rand(3, 3, 3)

print(x)

x = np.random.rand(2, 2, 2, 2, 2)

print(x)
```

Run the code snippet and see the output yourself.

6.8 Array Manipulation Routines

Let's have a look at ndarray manipulation routines. We can demonstrate these routines effectively with one dimensional and two dimensional ndarrays,

```
import numpy as np

x = np.arange(6)

print(x)
```

This creates a one-dimensional ndarray that we can use for reshaping. We can reshape the array as follows,

```
y = x.reshape((3, 2))
```

```
print(y)
```

The output is as follows,

```
[[0 1]
 [2 3]
 [4 5]]
```

Even NumPy library has got a `reshape()` function. We can use it as follows,

```
x = np.array([[0, 1, 2], [3, 4, 5]], dtype = np.uint8)
y = np.reshape(x, 6)
print(y)
```

The outout is as follows,

[0 1 2 3 4 5]

`ravel()` and `flatten()` functions can also flatten matrices into arrays,

```
y = np.ravel(x)
```

```
print(y)
```

```
y = x.flatten()
```

```
print(y)
```

The output of both function calls will be the same as the earlier output,

```
[0 1 2 3 4 5]
```

We can use arguments with `flatten()` function. We can flatten them in C-style (row order) or F-style (column order) as follows,

```
y = x.flatten('C')
```

```
print(y)
```

```
y = x.flatten('F')
```

```
print(y)
```

Output is as follows respectively,

```
[0 1 2 3 4 5]
```

```
[0 3 1 4 2 5]
```

Let's understand how to stack two ndarrays, by creating two ndarrays.

```
x = np.array([1, 2, 3], dtype = np.uint8)
y = np.array([4, 5, 6], dtype = np.uint8)
```

We can stack the ndarrays as follows,

```
z = np.stack((x, y))

print(z)
```

The output is as follows,

```
[[1 2 3]
 [4 5 6]]
```

We can specify the axis too. For n dimensional arrays, the value of axis argument can range from –n to n as follows,

```
z = np.stack((x, y), axis=0)
print(z)
z = np.stack((x, y), axis=1)
print(z)
z = np.stack((x, y), axis=-1)
print(z)
```

The output is as follows,

```
[[1 2 3]
 [4 5 6]]

[[1 4]
 [2 5]
 [3 6]]

[[1 4]
 [2 5]
 [3 6]]
```

Similarly, we have dstack(), vstack(), and hstack() functions. Let's see their usage,

```
z = np.dstack((x, y))
print(z)
z = np.hstack((x, y))
print(z)
z = np.vstack((x, y))
print(z)
```

The respective outputs will be as follows,

```
[[[1 4]
  [2 5]
  [3 6]]]
[1 2 3 4 5 6]
[[1 2 3]
 [4 5 6]]
```

Let's have a look at split() function now. Following is the usage,

```
x = np.arange(9)

print(x)

a, b, c = np.split(x, 3)

print(a, b, c)
```

Following is the output,

```
[0 1 2 3 4 5 6 7 8]
[0 1 2] [3 4 5] [6 7 8]
```

As you can see, split() has split the ndarray into three equal parts. Let's have a look at few other versions of the same function. For that, I will use a 4 X 4 X 4 matrix. Also, I want you to run the code and see the output for yourself.

```
x = np.random.rand(4, 4, 4)
print(x)
```

```
y, z = np.split(x, 2)
print(y, z)
y, z = np.hsplit(x, 2)
print(y, z)
y, z = np.vsplit(x, 2)
print(y, z)
y, z = np.dsplit(x, 2)
print(y, z)
```

Let's see flip, roll, and rotate operations by using a two-dimensional matrix.

```
x = np.arange(16).reshape(4, 4)
print(x)
```

Following is the output,

```
[[ 0  1  2  3]
 [ 4  5  6  7]
 [ 8  9 10 11]
 [12 13 14 15]]
```

We can flip this ndarray with flip() function. Just like split(), we can use axis parameter and for n-dimensional array it ranges from –n to n.

```
y = np.flip(x, axis = -1)
print(y)
y = np.flip(x, axis = 0)
print(y)
y = np.flip(x, axis = 1)
print(y)
```

Following is the output,

```
[[ 3  2  1  0]
 [ 7  6  5  4]
 [11 10  9  8]
 [15 14 13 12]]
```

```
[[12 13 14 15]
 [ 8  9 10 11]
 [ 4  5  6  7]
 [ 0  1  2  3]]
[[ 3  2  1  0]
 [ 7  6  5  4]
 [11 10  9  8]
 [15 14 13 12]]
```

We can flip it from left to right and from up to down respective as follows,

```
y = np.fliplr(x)
print(y)
y = np.flipud(x)
print(y)
```

Following is the output,

```
[[ 0  1  2  3]
 [ 4  5  6  7]
 [ 8  9 10 11]
 [12 13 14 15]]

[[ 0  1  2  3]
 [ 4  5  6  7]
 [ 8  9 10 11]
 [12 13 14 15]]
```

We can also roll and rotate the ndarray as follows,

```
y = np.roll(x, 8)
print(y)
y = np.rot90(x)
print(y)
```

The output is as follows,

```
[[ 8  9 10 11]
 [12 13 14 15]
```

```
[ 0  1  2  3]
[ 4  5  6  7]]

[[ 3  7 11 15]
 [ 2  6 10 14]
 [ 1  5  9 13]
 [ 0  4  8 12]]
```

6.9 Bitwise and Statistical Operations

Let's generate two ndarrays with the binary values only and see the bitwise operations,

```
x = np.array([0, 1, 0, 1], np.uint8)
y = np.array([0, 0, 1, 1], np.uint8)

print(np.bitwise_and(x, y))
print(np.bitwise_or(x, y))
print(np.bitwise_xor(x, y))
print(np.bitwise_not(x))
```

The code above is self-explanatory. The following is the output,

```
[0 0 0 1]
[0 1 1 1]
[0 1 1 0]
[255 254 255 254]
```

We can also use various statistical functions. Run the code below and see the output for yourself.

```
a = np.random.randint(low = 0, high = 10, size = 10)
print(np.median(a))
print(np.average(a))
print(np.mean(a))
print(np.std(a))
```

```
print(np.var(a))
print(np.histogram(a))
```

6.10 Summary

In this chapter, we got introduced to the NumPy and ndarrays. We also learned the basics of matplotlib. We saw ndarray creation and manipulation routines in detail. We will learn matplotlib in detail in the next chapter.

Exercise

As an exercise to this chapter, visit all the URLs in the chapter. Also, we have explain the demonstrations of all the functions for two dimensional arrays mostly. I want you to try them with three or more dimensional arrays as inputs.

CHAPTER 7
Visualization with Matplotlib

In the last chapter, we got started with programming. We have learned **NumPy** in detail. We have studied the ndarray data structure in detail and then learned to use NumPy's ndarray creation and modification routines in details. We also saw basic visualization with **matplotlib** library.

In this chapter, we will learn how to use **matplotlib** for plotting in detail.

7.1 Single Line Plots

Let's, begin with the simple types of visualizations. Initially, we will see how to plot a list with matplotlib. I am creating a new **Jupyter** notebook for every chapter. And, all these notebooks are available in the CD provided with this book. So, you can, too, create a new notebook for this and other chapters in the book. Add the following code to the notebook,

```
%matplotlib inline
import matplotlib.pyplot as plt
x = [1, 4, 5, 2, 3, 6]
plt.plot(x)
plt.show()
```

In the above code snippet, we are using the functions from `pyplot` package of matplotlib. `plt.plot()` function plots the given values. `plt.show()` displays all the figures, which are created by `plt.plot()`. Following is the output, *(figure 7.1)*

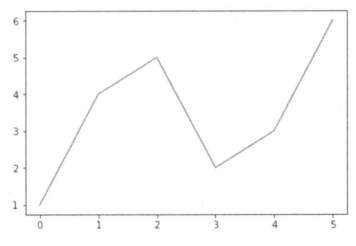

Figure 7.1 Simple graph

We can even pass a NumPy ndarray to the `plot()` function, as follows,

```
import numpy as np
x = np.arange(10)
plt.plot(x)
plt.show()
```

Following is the output, *(figure 7.2)*

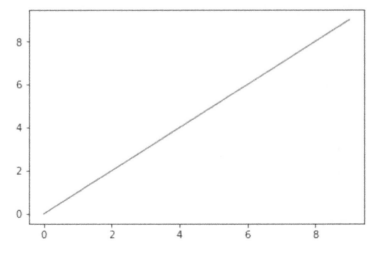

Figure 7.2 NumPy visualization

We can even pass pair of arguments for X axis and Y axis, as follows,

```
plt.plot(x, [y**2 for y in x])
plt.show()
```

Following is the output, *(figure 7.3)*

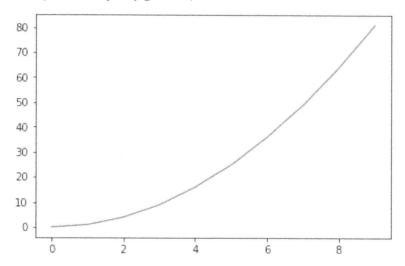

Figure 7.3 Squares of natural numbers visualized

We can simply, write the code above as,

```
plt.plot(x, x**2)
plt.show()
```

The output will be the same.

7.2 Multiline Plots

We can show multiple graphs in the same **matplotlib** window. We just need to use one `plot()` per graph. Following is the example,

```
%matplotlib inline
import numpy as np
import matplotlib.pyplot as plt
x = np.arange(10)
plt.plot(x, x**2)
plt.plot(x, x**3)
```

```
plt.plot(x, x*2)
plt.plot(x, 2**x)
plt.show()
```

Following is the output, *(figure 7.4)*

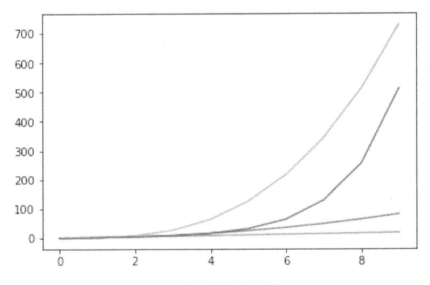

Figure 7.4 Multiline Plots

As you can see, **matplotlib** automatically assigns different colors to different graphs. We can do the same with a single `plot()` function call. Following is the code,

```
plt.plot(x, x**2, x, x**3, x, x*2, x, 2**x)
plt.show()
```

The code above produces the same output, as earlier code example produces.

We can use NumPy ndarrays for multiline plots, as follows,

```
x = np.array([[1, 2, 6, 3], [4, 5, 3, 2]])
plt.plot(x)
plt.show()
```

Following is the output, *(figure 7.5)*

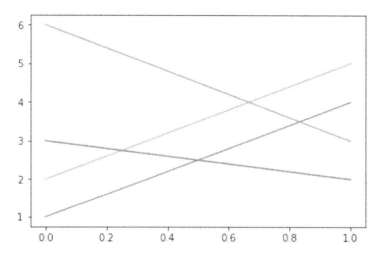

Figure 7.5 Multiline Plots with NumPy

We can plot multiline visualizations with random data too, as follow,

```
data = np.random.randn(2, 10)
print(data)
plt.plot(data[0], data[1])
plt.show()
```

Following is the output, *(figure 7.6)*

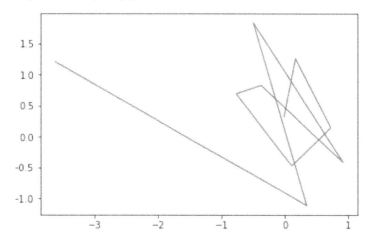

Figure 7.6 Multiline plots with NumPy random data

7.3 Grid, Axes, and Labels

Till now, we have seen the plain graph with default settings. In this section, we will understand how to enable grid, change axes, and add labels. Let's enable the grid now,

```
%matplotlib inline
import numpy as np
import matplotlib.pyplot as plt
x = np.arange(3)
plt.plot(x, x**2, x, x**3, x, 2*x, x, 2**x)
plt.grid(True)
print(plt.axis())
plt.show()
```

The program, above, enables grid in the visualization. And, the statement `plt.axis()` returns the limits of X and Y axes. Following the output, *(figure 7.7)*

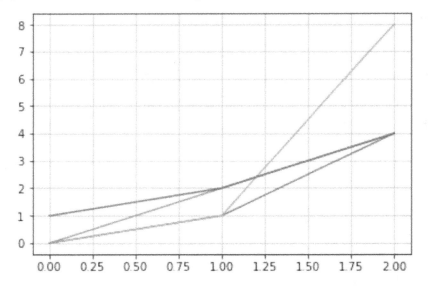

Figure 7.7 Enabling the grid and printing the limits of X and Y axes

Also, we can use same `plt.axis()` function call to set the limits of the X and Y axes. Following is the code example,

```
x = np.arange(3)
```

```
plt.plot(x, x**2, x, x**3, x, 2*x, x, 2**x)
plt.grid(True)
plt.axis([0, 2, 0, 8])
plt.show()
```

Following is the output, *(figure 7.8)*

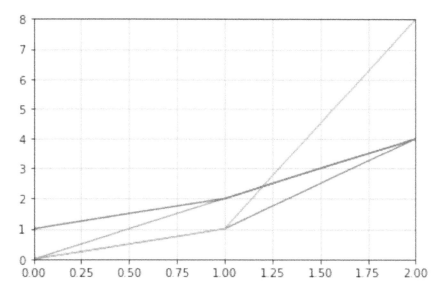

Figure 7.8 Setting the limits of X and Y axes

We can, also, use `plt.xlim()` and `plt.ylim()` functions to set the limits of X and Y axes, respectively. The code is, as follows,

```
x = np.arange(3)
plt.plot(x, x**2, x, x**3, x, 2*x, x, 2**x)
plt.grid(True)
plt.xlim([0, 2])
plt.ylim([0, 8])
plt.show()
```

The above code produces the same output, as the earlier code example.

We can set the labels for X and Y axes and title of the visualizations, as follows,

```
x = np.arange(3)
```

```
plt.plot(x, x**2, x, x**3, x, 2*x, x, 2**x)
plt.grid(True)
plt.xlabel('x = np.arange(3)')
plt.xlim([0, 2])
plt.ylabel('y = f(x)')
plt.ylim([0, 8])
plt.title('Simple Plot Demo')
plt.show()
```

Following is the output, *(figure 7.9)*

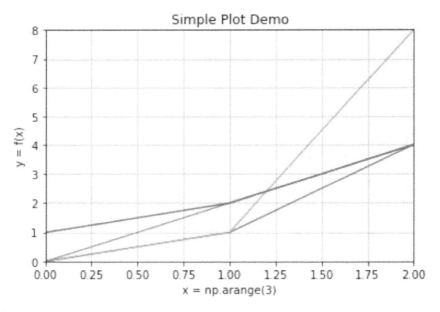

Figure 7.9 Setting the axes labels and title

We can add legends in the visualizations by adding `label` parameter in the `plot()` function call, as follows,

```
x = np.arange(3)
plt.plot(x, x**2, label='x**2')
plt.plot(x, x**3, label='x**3')
plt.plot(x, 2*x, label='2*x')
plt.plot(x, 2**x, label='2**x')
plt.legend()
```

```
plt.grid(True)
plt.xlabel('x = np.arange(3)')
plt.xlim([0, 2])
plt.ylabel('y = f(x)')
plt.ylim([0, 8])
plt.title('Simple Plot Demo')
plt.show()
```

Following is the output, where you can see the legend at the default position (top-left corner), *(figure 7.10)*

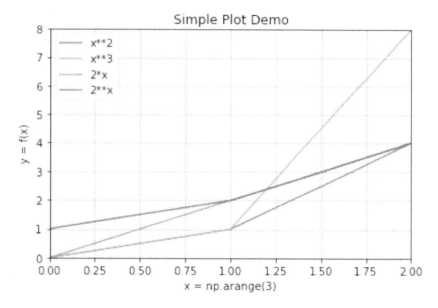

Figure 7.10 Legends

We can use `plt.legend()` function to define the labels too, as follows,

```
x = np.arange(3)
plt.plot(x, x**2, x, x**3, x, 2*x, x, 2**x)
plt.legend(['x**2', 'x**3', '2*x', '2**x'])
plt.grid(True)
plt.xlabel('x = np.arange(3)')
plt.xlim([0, 2])
plt.ylabel('y = f(x)')
plt.ylim([0, 8])
```

```
plt.title('Simple Plot Demo')
plt.show()
```

The above code produces the same output as the earlier code example.

We can, also, set the location of the legend box by adding `loc` parameter to `plt.legend()` function, as follows,

```
x = np.arange(3)
plt.plot(x, x**2, x, x**3, x, 2*x, x, 2**x)
plt.legend(['x**2', 'x**3', '2*x', '2**x'], loc='upper
center')
plt.grid(True)
plt.xlabel('x = np.arange(3)')
plt.xlim([0, 2])
plt.ylabel('y = f(x)')
plt.ylim([0, 8])
plt.title('Simple Plot Demo')
plt.show()
```

Following is the output, *(figure 7.11)*

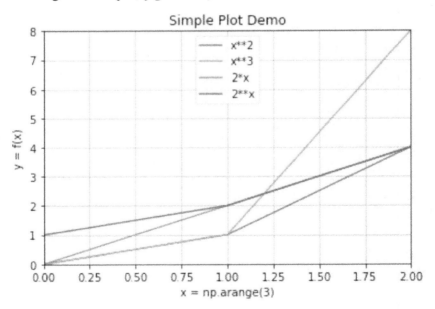

Figure 7.11 Legend box in center

We can, also, save the figure with `plt.savefig()`, as follows,

```
x = np.arange(3)
plt.plot(x, x**2, x, x**3, x, 2*x, x, 2**x)
plt.legend(['x**2', 'x**3', '2*x', '2**x'], loc='upper
center')
plt.grid(True)
plt.xlabel('x = np.arange(3)')
plt.xlim([0, 2])
plt.ylabel('y = f(x)')
plt.ylim([0, 8])
plt.title('Simple Plot Demo')
plt.savefig('test.png')
plt.show()
```

When we execute the above code, we get the output visualization saved in the current directory from where the **Jupyter** notebook is launched from in the command prompt.

7.4 Colors, Styles, and Markers

We can play a lot with colors. Let's see how we can draw lines with various colors. The code is, as follows,

```
%matplotlib inline
import matplotlib.pyplot as plt
import numpy as np
x = np.arange(5)
y = x
plt.plot(x, y+1, 'g')
plt.plot(x, y+0.5, 'y')
plt.plot(x, y, 'r')
plt.plot(x, y-0.2, 'c')
plt.plot(x, y-0.4, 'k')
plt.plot(x, y-0.6, 'm')
plt.plot(x, y-0.8, 'w')
plt.plot(x, y-1, 'b')
plt.show()
```

The above code draws parallel lines with various colors, as shown in figure 7.12.

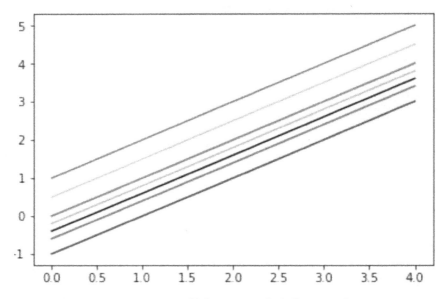

Figure 7.12 Parallel Lines with different colors

We can achieve the same result with a single `plt.plot()` function call, as follows,

```
plt.plot(x, y+1, 'g', x, y+0.5, 'y', x, y, 'r', x,
y-0.2, 'c',
            x, y-0.4, 'k', x, y-0.6, 'm', x, y-0.8, 'w',
x, y-1, 'b')

plt.show()
```

The above code produces the same output, as the earlier code example.

We have, mostly, been using the default line style till now. Now, we will see various line styles. The code is, as follows,

```
plt.plot(x, y, '-', x, y+1, '--', x, y+2, '-.', x,
y+3, ':')
plt.show()
```

The above code draws parallel lines with different line styles, as follows, *(figure 7.13)*

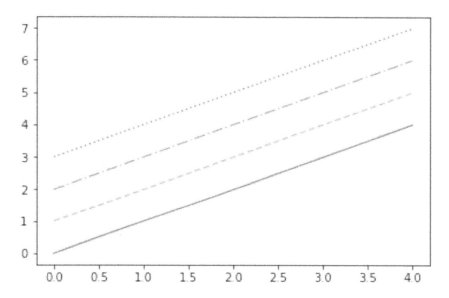

Figure 7.13 Parallel Lines with different line styles

We can, also, have different markers for visualizations. The code is, as follows,

```
plt.plot(x, y, '.')
plt.plot(x, y+0.5, ',')
plt.plot(x, y+1, 'o')
plt.plot(x, y+2, '<')
plt.plot(x, y+3, '>')
plt.plot(x, y+4, 'v')
plt.plot(x, y+5, '^')
plt.plot(x, y+6, '1')
plt.plot(x, y+7, '2')
plt.plot(x, y+8, '3')
plt.plot(x, y+9, '4')
plt.plot(x, y+10, 's')
plt.plot(x, y+11, 'p')
plt.plot(x, y+12, '*')
plt.plot(x, y+13, 'h')
plt.plot(x, y+14, 'H')
plt.plot(x, y+15, '+')
```

```
plt.plot(x, y+16, 'D')
plt.plot(x, y+17, 'd')
plt.plot(x, y+18, '|')
plt.plot(x, y+19, '_')
plt.show()
```

Following is the output, of the code above, *(figure 7.14)*

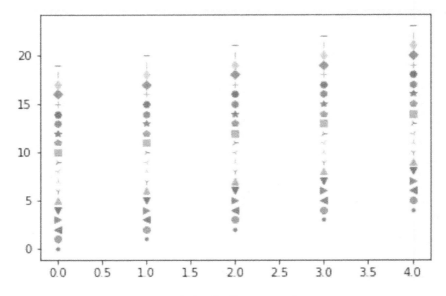

Figure 7.14 Different markers

We have not mentioned any line style, that's why only markers are visible. Now, let us combine color, line style, and marker. We have to pass line color, marker, and line style in that order in a single argument as shown in the code below,

```
plt.plot(x, y, 'mo--')
plt.plot(x, y+1 , 'g*-.')
plt.show()
```

The output is, as follows, *(figure 7.15)*

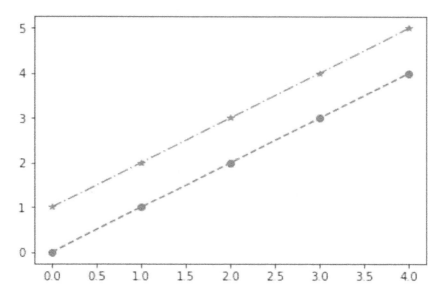

Figure 7.15 Combining markers, line styles, and line colors

We can customize any visualization even further, as follows,

```
plt.plot(x, y, color='g', linestyle='--',
linewidth=1.5,
        marker='^', markerfacecolor='b',
markeredgecolor='k',
        markeredgewidth=1.5, markersize=5)
plt.grid(True)
plt.show()
```

Following is the output, *(figure 7.16)*

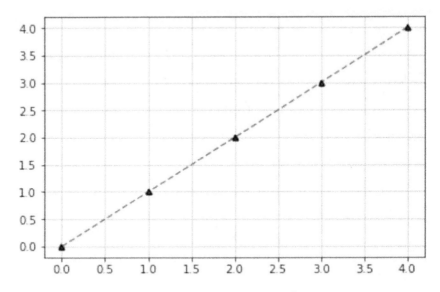

Figure 7.16 Customizing visualization

We can even change the values on the X and Y axes scales with `plt.xticks()` and `plt.yticks()` functions, as follows,

```
x = y = np.arange(10)
plt.plot(x, y, 'o--')
plt.xticks(range(len(x)), ['a', 'b', 'c', 'd', 'e',
'f', 'g', 'h', 'i', 'j'])
plt.yticks(range(1, 10, 1))
plt.show()
```

The code above produces customized scales of X and Y axes, as follows, *(figure 7.17)*

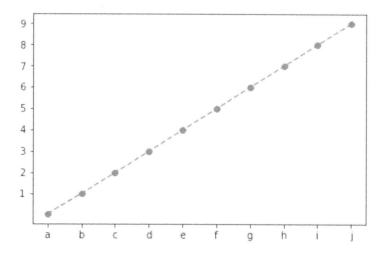

Figure 7.17 Customizing X and Y axes scales

7.5 Summary

In this long chapter, we have seen the most used features in **matplotlib** library in detail. We will be frequently using these features very frequently throughout the book. In the next chapter, we will study and implement many important image processing concepts with **NumPy** and **matplotlib** libraries.

CHAPTER 8

Basic Image Processing with NumPy and Matplotlib

In the last chapter, we have learned how to modify the default settings of visualizations of matplotlib. We also have studied multiline and single-line plots, in detail. We saw how to visualize NumPy data with matplotlib. We, also, have experimented with colors, line styles, and markers.

Now, we know NumPy and Matplotlib and can comfortably work with them. We have covered all the required topics needed to get started with image processing. So, in this chapter, we will learn the basic image processing concepts and implement them with NumPy and matplotlib.

8.1 Image Datasets

As, we are going to learn the topic of **image processing**, we will need a lot of test images. You can use any of the image. You can, even, capture them with digital camera or scan the printed film photographs from your family archives. However, the best option is to use the standard sets of photographs, used by the worldwide community of image processing researchers. You can find such sets at the following URLs,

http://sipi.usc.edu/database/

http://www.imageprocessingplace.com/root_files_V3/image_databases.htm

Also, University of Tsukuba (http://www.tsukuba.ac.jp/en/) has got excellent set of images for advanced image processing and computer vision operations. Following is the URL for their stereo dataset,

http://www.cvlab.cs.tsukuba.ac.jp/dataset/tsukubastereo.php

You can, also, find other datasets there.

So, download the test images from these URLs and store them in a local directory of your computer or Pi. We will be using them throughout the chapter and the rest of the book as test images.

8.2 Installing Pillow

We need **Python Imaging Library (PIL)** for reading images that are not in PNG format, using matplotlib (we're going to see it next). However, its development appears to be discontinued and there is a newer version of it known as **pillow,** which is under active development. We can check more details about it, at https://pillow.readthedocs.io/en/stable/. We run the following command to install it on Windows,

```
pip3 install pillow
```

We run the following command on terminal to install it on Raspberry Pi,

```
sudo pip3 install pillow
```

8.3 Reading and saving images

Let's start with reading, displaying, and saving images with matplotlib. First, import all the required libraries and enable matplotlib visualization with the magic command, as follows,

```
%matplotlib inline
import numpy as np
import matplotlib.pyplot as plt
```

We can read image into a variable, as follows,

```
img1 = plt.imread('/home/pi/Dataset/4.1.06.tiff')
```

Note, that, the above code is for Linux and Raspberry Pi. For Windows OS, the code will be, as follows,

```
img1 = plt.imread('D:\\Dataset\\4.1.06.tiff')
```

I will, mostly, be using a Windows computer for the programming. However, the code, when we make appropriate changes for Linux platform, works well with Raspberry Pi Raspbian OS well.

We have to use `plt.imshow()` function, followed by `plt.show()`, to visualize the image,

```
plt.imshow(img1)
```

```
plt.axis('off')
plt.title('Tree')
plt.show()
```

This will show a color image, as it is. However, when it comes to the greyscale images then it's a bit tricky. Greyscale images are shown, with a default colormap. Following is an example code that reads and displays a grayscale image,

```
img1 = plt.imread('D:\\Dataset\\5.3.01.tiff')
plt.imshow(img1)
plt.axis('off')
plt.show()
```

The output is as follows, *(figure 8.1)*

Figure 8.1 A greyscale image rendered with default colormap

As you can see that the greyscale image is tinted. We can avoid this by applying grey colormap, as follows,

```
img1 = plt.imread('D:\\Dataset\\5.3.01.tiff')
plt.imshow(img1, cmap='gray')
plt.axis('off')
plt.show()
```

Run the above program and you will see the greyscale image without tinting.

We can save the image to a location on a disk, as follows,

```
plt.imsave('/home/pi/output.png', img1)
```

For windows, it will be,

```
plt.imsave('D:\\output.png', img1)
```

8.4 NumPy for Images

When, we use Python programming for image processing operations, all the images that's been used, are read and stored in memory (RAM), as NumPy ndarrays. We have already seen ndarrays and their properties. These properties have meaning when we work with ndarrays representing images. Let's see the example. Following are the properties of a color image,

```
img1 = plt.imread('D:\\Dataset\\4.1.06.tiff')
print(type(img1))
print(img1.shape)
print(img1.ndim)
print(img1.size)
print(img1.dtype)
print(img1.nbytes)
```

Following is the output,

```
<class 'numpy.ndarray'>
(256, 256, 3)
3
196608
uint8
196608
```

Let's, analyze it, one by one. The first output confirms that the image is indeed represented as a NumPy array. The property `shape` returns the shape of image. In the returned tuple, first two numbers represent width and height, respectively, (i.e. resolution). The last number in the tuple represents the number of color channels. For all the color image, it will mostly be 3 or 4. The property `ndim` represents the number of dimensions. It is 3, for a color image, and 2, for a greyscale image. The property `size` is the size of the image, which means how many data points or numbers it takes to represent the image. If you multiply all the numbers in the tuple returned by the property `shape`, it is exactly the same number.

The property dtype tells us how we are representing each data point for the image. Here, we are using uint8 which means unsigned integer of 8 bits (1 byte). Finally, nbytes tell us how many bytes are required to store it in memory (RAM). It is the multiplication of the size and the memory required for the given datatype, in which, image data points are represented. Here, uint8 takes 1 byte each and the size is 196608, thus, the number of bytes required are 196608 x 1 = 196608.

Let's do the same for a greyscale image,

```
img2 = plt.imread('D:\\Dataset\\5.3.01.tiff')
print(type(img2))
print(img2.shape)
print(img2.ndim)
print(img2.size)
print(img2.dtype)
print(img2.nbytes)
```

Following is, the output,

```
<class 'numpy.ndarray'>
(1024, 1024)
2
1048576
uint8
1048576
```

The property shape will return a tuple with two numbers that refers to resolution of the image. There is only one channel in any greyscale image that stores the intensity values of the grey color, for all the pixels, in the image. Thus, the number of dimensions, the property ndim, is 2. The image data points are still represented with uint8. Rest of the two properties are dependent on these three properties and can be deduced, once we have these three values.

We can access value for individual channel in a color image, as follow,

```
print(img1[10, 10, 0])
print(img1[10, 10, 1])
print(img1[10, 10, 2])
```

The code above returns the values for channel 0, channel 1, and channel 2 at pixel 10, 10, as follows,

```
199
216
220
```

We can even use the slicing operation, as follows,

```
print(img1[10, 10, :])
```

Output is, as follows,

```
[199 216 220]
```

For a greyscale image, we can know the value of individual pixel, as follows,

```
print(img2[10, 10])
```

The output is,

```
71
```

8.5 Image Statistics

We can retrieve the image statistics with the NumPy ndarray properties, as follows,

```
img1 = plt.imread('D:\\Dataset\\4.1.06.tiff')
print(img1.min())
print(img1.max())
print(img1.mean())
```

Run the above code and check the output. **NumPy** has some statistical functions to retrieve statistics of a NumPy array. Following are those functions,

```
print(np.median(img1))
print(np.average(img1))
print(np.mean(img1))
print(np.std(img1))
print(np.var(img1))
```

Run the above code and check the output.

8.6 Image Masks

We can create the **masks** for the images to cover the images with pixels of a particular color. Following is the code sample,

```
img1 = plt.imread('D:\\Dataset\\4.1.06.tiff')
nrows, ncols, channels = img1.shape
row, col = np.ogrid[:nrows, :ncols]
cnt_row, cnt_col = nrows/2, ncols/2
outer_disk_mask = ((row - cnt_row) ** 2 + (col - cnt_
col) ** 2 > (nrows/2) ** 2)
img1.setflags(write=1)
img1[outer_disk_mask]=0
plt.imshow(img1)
plt.axis('off')
plt.title('Masked Image')
plt.show()
```

In the above code, initially, we are creating an outer disk mask and, then, setting all the pixels in the mask to the value 0 (0 means black). The function `setflags(write=1)` allows us to modify the pixels in the image stored in memory (**RAM**). Following is the output, *(figure 8.2)*

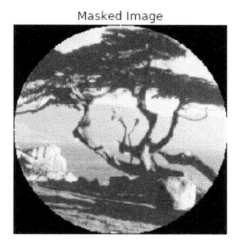

Figure 8.2 Masked image

8.7 Image Channels

We know that, for colored images, the information to the colors is saved in separate channels. There are many schemes to do that. When `plt.imread()` reads a color image, it stores the color information in NumPy array, such that, the information for colors red, green, and blue is stored in color channels separately. It can be retrieved by slicing the NumPy array that stores the color image, as follows,

```
img1 = plt.imread('D:\\Dataset\\4.1.04.tiff')


r = img1[:, :, 0]
g = img1[:, :, 1]
b = img1[:, :, 2]

output = [img1, r, g, b]

titles = ['Image', 'Red', 'Green', 'Blue']

for i in range(4):
    plt.subplot(2, 2, i+1)

    plt.axis('off')
    plt.title(titles[i])
    if i == 0:
        plt.imshow(output[i])
    else:
        plt.imshow(output[i], cmap='gray')

plt.show()
```

In the above code, we are retrieving the information for color channels in the separate two-dimensional ndarray for each color. So, we have 3 different two-dimensional ndarrays with datatype uint8. We know that an unsigned integer of 8 bit can store 256 values ranging from 0 to 255. Each value represents an intensity level for that particular color. A **pixel** is made of information related to 3 color channels. Thus, a pixel can have any one of the possible 256 x 256 x 256 = 16777216 color values. That is, around 16 and half million colors. Human eye can distinguish around 10 million colors. So, this 3-byte representation of a color pixel is adequate for humans. The output of the code above is as follows,

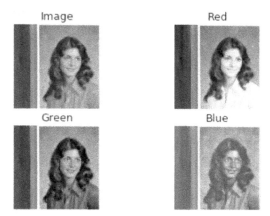

Figure 8.3 Separated color channels

As you can see, we are able to separate and display the color channels. *(figure 8.3)*

Also, if you have noticed, we are displaying multiple images in matplotlib output. This is possible due to `subplot()` function. This function allows us to treat the output, as a grid and set the output images in that grid. The first two arguments passed to `subplot()` to convey size of the grid. In this example, it is 2 x 2. The last argument passed conveys the position of the image in this grid. The top left position is **1**, the horizontally adjacent position is **2,** and so on. This is very useful, as we will be using the same template of code to display multiple images in a single output, throughout the book. We can even show multiple plots separately this way. We will see that too in this book.

We can even recombine them to form original image, as follows,

```
output = np.dstack((r, g, b))
plt.imshow(output)
plt.show()
```

Run the above code and verify, if the output is the original image.

8.8 Arithmetic Operations on Images

We can perform a lot of arithmetic operations on the images. For this section, I am not showing the output, in the book. Instead, I want you to run all the code examples below and check the outputs.

We have seen a lot of operations on NumPy arrays, in the earlier section. We are going to see the same operations, in this section, in the context of images. Choose two images of same size resolution and dimension from the image dataset that's been downloaded. Following is the sample code,

```
img1 = plt.imread('D:\\Dataset\\4.1.06.tiff')
img2 = plt.imread('D:\\Dataset\\4.1.04.tiff')
plt.imshow(img1)
plt.show()
plt.imshow(img2)
plt.show()
```

We can add two images, as follows,

```
plt.imshow(img1 + img2)
plt.show()
```

We know that the addition operation over numbers is commutative. Changing position of operands does not change the final result. So, following is the equivalent of the above,

```
plt.imshow(img1 + img2)
plt.show()
```

We can subtract one image from the other, as follows,

```
plt.imshow(img1 - img2)
plt.show()
```

We, also, know that the subtraction operation is not commutative. So, the following code produces different output,

```
plt.imshow(img2 - img1)
plt.show()
```

We can flip the image, as follows,

```
plt.imshow(np.flip(img1, 0))
plt.show()
```

We can even change the axis of flip, as follows,

```
plt.imshow(np.flip(img1, 1))
plt.show()
```

We can roll the image, as follows,

```
plt.imshow(np.roll(img1, 2048))
plt.show()
```

We can flip the image from left to right, as follows,

```
plt.imshow(np.fliplr(img1))
plt.show()
```

We can even flip the image vertically,

```
plt.imshow(np.flipud(img1))
plt.show()
```

We can rotate the image, as follows,

```
plt.imshow(np.rot90(img1))
plt.show()
```

8.9 Bitwise Logical Operations

We can use NumPy bitwise logical operation functions on images. We know that all the bitwise logical operations are commutative. We will use same images that we used in the earlier section for the demonstration of logical operations. Following code demonstrates **bitwise logical AND** between images,

```
plt.imshow(np.bitwise_and(img1, img2))
plt.show()
```

Following is the code for bitwise logical OR operation,

```
plt.imshow(np.bitwise_or(img1, img2))
plt.show()
```

Bitwise logical XOR can be achieved, as follows,

```
plt.imshow(np.bitwise_xor(img2, img1))
plt.show()
```

Bitwise logical NOT is nothing but negative of an image, as follows,

```
plt.subplot(1, 2, 1)
plt.imshow(img1)
plt.subplot(1, 2, 2)
plt.imshow(np.bitwise_not(img1))
plt.show()
```

8.10 Image Histograms with NumPy and Matplotlib

In the last chapter, we saw the code for computing histogram of a NumPy ndarray. However, we did not discuss the concept in detail. I was saving it for this occasion when I can explain it in visual way. A **histogram** is a visual representation of distribution of data in a dataset. In simple words, it is visualization of frequency distribution table of a dataset. A **distribution table** is nothing, but a table of values in a dataset versus the number of occurrences of those values in that dataset. The **dataset**, here, is an image represented by NumPy ndarray. Let's create and visualize the chnnelwise histograms of a color image. The code is as follows,

```
img1 = plt.imread('D:\\Dataset\\4.1.01.tiff')
```

```
r = img1[:, :, 0]
g = img1[:, :, 1]
b = img1[:, :, 2]
```

In the above code, we are separating the channels, by slicing the NumPy array, that holds the image. Let's adjust the space between the subplots with the following code,

```
plt.subplots_adjust(hspace=0.5, wspace=0.5)
```

Now let's plot the original image,

```
plt.subplot(2, 2, 1)
plt.title('Original Image')
plt.imshow(img1)
```

Now, let's compute the histogram for the red channel,

```
hist, bins = np.histogram(r.ravel(), bins=256,
range=(0, 256))
```

The red channel is a two dimensional NumPy ndarray. First, we are flattening it and passing it, as an argument, to `np.histogram()` function. We are, also, mentioning the number of bins and range of the values for which the histogram is to be computed. Finally, we will use `plt.bar()` to show the histogram visually,

```
plt.subplot(2, 2, 2)
plt.title('Red Histogram')
plt.bar(bins[:-1], hist)
```

Same way, we can compute and visualize the histograms for other channels as follows,

```
hist, bins = np.histogram(g.ravel(), bins=256,
range=(0, 256))
plt.subplot(2, 2, 3)
plt.title('Green Histogram')
plt.bar(bins[:-1], hist)

hist, bins = np.histogram(b.ravel(), bins=256,
range=(0, 256))
plt.subplot(2, 2, 4)
plt.title('Blue Histogram')
plt.bar(bins[:-1], hist)

plt.show()
```

The output is as follows, *(figure 8.4)*

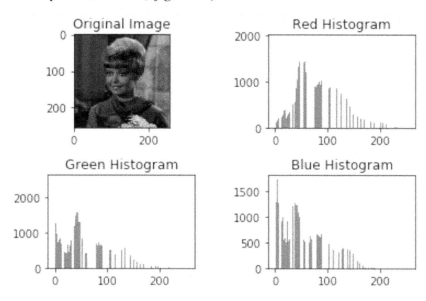

Figure 8.4 Channelwise histograms for a color image

We can directly use `plt.hist()` function in matplotlib to compute and visualize histogram, as follows,

```
plt.subplots_adjust(hspace=0.5, wspace=0.5)
plt.subplot(2, 2, 1)
plt.title('Original Image')
plt.imshow(img1)
plt.subplot(2, 2, 2)
plt.title('Red Histogram')
plt.hist(r.ravel(), bins=256, range=(0, 256))
plt.subplot(2, 2, 3)
plt.title('Green Histogram')
plt.hist(g.ravel(), bins=256, range=(0, 256))
plt.subplot(2, 2, 4)
plt.title('Blue Histogram')
plt.hist(b.ravel(), bins=256, range=(0, 256))
plt.show()
```

The output of the code, above, will exactly be the same as the output of the earlier code.

This is how we can compute and visualize the histogram of any image or NumPy ndarray.

8.11 Summary

In this chapter, we have studied the image processing operations on images with **NumPy** and **matplotlib**. We have not worked with any image processing library yet. **NumPy** itself can be used for most basic operations on images. We can even implement our own functions for various image processing operations. We will do the same in the next chapter. We will study a few advanced image processing operations and write a few functions, on our own, to perform those few image processing operations with **NumPy** and **matplotlib** only.

Exercise

We have seen the demonstration of various image processing techniques for the color images. I want you to perform all these image processing operations for greyscale images. It will be an interesting exercise.

CHAPTER 9

Advanced Image Processing with NumPy and Matplotlib

In the last chapter, we have got started with the image processing programming. We have learned how to implement basic image processing operations with **NumPy** and **matplotlib**. We have studied and implemented very basic operations, without using any dedicated library for image processing.

We will continue with the image processing operations with **NumPy** and **matplotlib**. We will study a bit more advanced operations and we will write the functions for them, ourselves. We will study the concepts like thresholding, color to greyscale, normalization, and other operations.

9.1 Color to Greyscale Conversion

We know that a color image has 3 channels and it is represented with **RGB** colorspace. We can convert a color image to a greyscale image. We need to convert values represented by 3 channels to a single channel. First, we import all the required libraries, following is the code:

```
%matplotlib inline
import numpy as np
import matplotlib.pyplot as plt
```

The custom function to **convert** color image to greyscale image, as follows:

```
def rgb2gray(img):
    r = img[:, :, 0]
    g = img[:, :, 1]
    b = img[:, :, 2]
    return (0.2989 * r
```

```
+0.5870 * g
+0.1140 * b)
```

Let's see, the effect of this function on the shape of a color image, after applying it:

```
img = plt.imread('D:\\Dataset\\4.2.03.tiff')
print(img.shape)
print(rgb2gray(img).shape)
```

The output is as follows:

```
(512, 512, 3)
(512, 512)
```

For verifying it visually, we can show it in the **Jupyter** notebook:

```
plt.subplot(1, 2, 1)
plt.imshow(img)
plt.subplot(1, 2, 2)
plt.imshow(rgb2gray(img), cmap='gray')
plt.show()
```

Run the code written above and check the output.

9.2 Image Thresholding

Let's learn an important concept, known as, **image thresholding**. **Image thresholding** is the most basic type of image segmentation. **Image segmentation** refers to partitioning an image into multiple segments. **Segmented image** is easier to analyze and we can extract various features from segmented image.

Thresholding refers to converting an image into two parts, a **background** and a **foreground**. Thresholding works best on greyscale image. After thresholding, a greyscale image is converted into a black and white image, which is also called a **binary image**. Thresholding operation can be defined as a function, such that, it returns **255**, when the input value is greater than the threshold, else it returns **0**. Following is a custom defined threshold function and an inverted threshold function:

```
def threshold(img, thresh=127):
    return((img > thresh) * 255).astype("uint8")

def inverted_threshold(img, thresh=127):
    return((img < thresh) * 255).astype("uint8")
```

In the function above, the default threshold value is **127**. Let's choose a greyscale image for demonstration:

```
img = plt.imread('D:\\Dataset\\5.1.11.tiff')
plt.imshow(img, cmap='gray')
plt.show()
```

Following is the image: *(figure 9.1)*

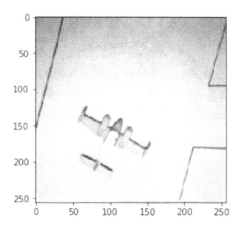

Figure 9.1 Test greyscale image

Following is the code to **test the greyscale images**:

```
plt.imshow(threshold(img), cmap='gray')
plt.show()
```

Following is the **thresholded** image: *(figure 9.2)*

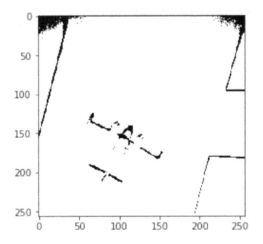

Figure 9.2 Thresholded image

Let's **test** the code with **custom threshold**, as follows,

```
plt.imshow(threshold(img, 200), cmap='gray')
plt.show()
```

Following is the output: *(figure 9.3)*

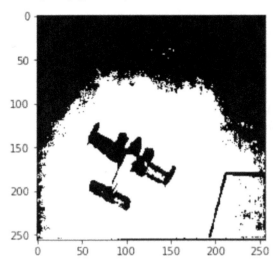

Figure 9.3 Thresholded image with threshold equals 200

We can use following code for **inverted threshold:**

```
plt.imshow(inverted_threshold(img), cmap='gray')
plt.show()
```

Also, for **custom threshold value**:

```
plt.imshow(inverted_threshold(img, 200), cmap='gray')
plt.show()
```

9.3 Tinting Color Images

We can write a custom function to tint color images. We will first load a color image in a variable and we will use this image to demonstrate the image processing operations in the next few sections:

```
img = plt.imread('D:\\Dataset\\4.1.01.tiff')
plt.imshow(img)
plt.show()
```

Let's define a function for **tinting** an image:

```
def tint(img, percent=0.5):
    return (img + (np.ones(img.shape) - img) *
percent).astype("uint8")
```

This function can be tested, as follows:

```
plt.axis('off')
plt.imshow(tint(img))
plt.show()
```

We can test it with **custom percentage for tinting,** as follows:

```
plt.axis('off')
plt.imshow(tint(img, 0.1))
plt.show()
```

Run the codes and check the output.

9.4 Shading Color Images

We can **shade** an image with the following function:

```
def shade(img, percent=0.5):
    return (img * (1 - percent)).astype("uint8")
```

We can demonstrate **shading with default percentage**, as follows:

```
plt.axis('off')
plt.imshow(shade(img))
plt.show()
```

We can test it with **custom percentage** for shading, as follows:

```
plt.axis('off')
plt.imshow(shade(img, 0.3))
plt.show()
```

9.5 Gradient

We can apply **gradient** on the images. The custom function, for that, is as follows:

```
def gradient(img, reverse=False):
    cols = img.shape[1]
    if reverse:
        C = np.linspace(1, 0, cols)
    else:
        C = np.linspace(0, 1, cols)
    C = np.dstack((C, C, C))
    print(C.shape)
    return (C * img).astype("uint8")
```

In the function above, we are multiplying the custom gradient C with the image for all the three channels of input image. We can even multiply the reverse gradient with image based on the input. Following is the example of the test code of the function:

```
plt.imshow(gradient(img))
plt.show()
```

Following is the example of **reverse gradient**:

```
plt.imshow(gradient(img, True))
plt.show()
```

9.6 Max RGB Filter

We can create a **max RGB filter** ourselves with **NumPy**. In **max RGB filter,** we compare the intensities of the all the channels of a color image for every pixel and keep the intensity of the channel with maximum intensity, as it is, and reduce the intensities of all the other channels to zero, for every pixel, in the image. Suppose, for a particular pixel the values of **RGB** are **(10, 200, 240)**, then after passing it through **max RGB filter** the pixel will have **RGB** values as **(0, 0, 240)**. Let's implement this function, as follows:

```
def max_rgb(img):
    r = img[:, :, 0]
    g = img[:, :, 1]
    b = img[:, :, 2]

    M = np.maximum(np.maximum(r, g), b)

    img.setflags(write=1)

    r[r < M] = 0
    g[g < M] = 0
    b[b < M] = 0

    return(np.dstack((r, g, b)))
```

We can apply the **filter** on any color image, as follows:

```
plt.imshow(max_rgb(img))
plt.show()
```

Run the code written above and check the result.

9.7 Intensity Normalization

We can also **normalize** the **intensity** of an image. Following is the code for the definition of the function:

```
def normalize(img):
```

```
lmin = float(img.min())
lmax = float(img.max())
return np.floor((img-lmin)/(lmax-lmin)*255.0)
```

We can use a greyscale image as a test image as follow:

```
img = plt.imread('D:\\Dataset\\7.2.01.tiff')
plt.imshow(img, cmap='gray')
plt.show()
```

Finally, we can **normalize** the chosen the **greyscale image,** as follows:

```
plt.imshow(normalize(img), cmap='gray')
plt.show()
```

9.8 Summary

We have studied a few advanced image processing concepts in this chapter. We, also, have implemented them without using any special library for image processing. This way almost all the popular image processing libraries use **NumPy** to implement the functionality for image processing and computer vision. From the next chapter onwards, we will start exploring one such dedicated image processing library, **scikit-image.**

Exercise

Many of the functions are implemented in this chapter, need specific types of images (greyscale or color) as input. Add the check in the beginning of definition of functions, where it will be checked, if the passed argument is the expected type of image. If it is not, then raise an exception and print an error message.

## CHAPTER 10

Getting Started with Scikit-Image

In the last two chapters, we got started with image processing with **NumPy** and **matplotlib**. In this chapter, we will have an introduction to scikit-image library which is a dedicated library for image processing and computer vision. We will have an introduction to the scikit project too. We will learn how to setup Windows PC and Raspberry Pi for image processing with scikit-image. Then, we will have a look at a few simple operations offered by the library.

10.1 Introduction to Scikits

Scikits stand for SciPy toolkits. These libraries are not the part of core **SciPy** library. They are hosted, developed, and maintained independently from core SciPy libraries. You can find out more about **scikits** at https://www.scipy.org/scikits.html and http://scikits.appspot.com/scikits. **Scikit-image** is a scikit and it specializes in image processing and computer vision. All the scikits heavily use **NumPy** and **SciPy** for implementation of various functionalities.

10.2 Installation of Scikit-learn on Windows and Raspberry pi Raspbian

Scikit-image requires cython package and cython requires a C++ compiler. For windows, we need to install the latest version **Microsoft Visual C++ Redistributable**. We can find it at https://visualstudio.microsoft.com/downloads. Download the setup file appropriate for your Windows (32 bit or 64 bit). Install the **VC++** redistributable by executing the setup file. Once done, open the command prompt and run the following command,

```
pip3 install scipy cython scikit-image
```

Raspberry Pi Raspbian and the other distributions of Linux already have gcc for C++. So, we can directly install required libraries. Just run the following command in terminal of Raspberry Pi,

```
sudo pip3 install scipy cython scikit-image
```

10.3 Basics of Scikit-image

Now, we will see the basics of **scikit-image**. Just like **matplotlib**, skikit-image has function imread(), imshow(), and show() to read and display images. They work exactly same as their counterparts in **matplotlib**. Following is the sample program to demonstrate the functionality of these functions,

```
%matplotlib inline
import skimage.io as io
img = io.imread('D:\\Dataset\\4.2.05.tiff')
print(type(img))
io.imshow(img)
io.show()
```

The code above reads and displays an image. We are using `io` module of scikit-image for that. In this section, we will go through this module in detail.

Scikit-image has many images in the data module which we can use to demonstrate image processing operations. We can use the images in the `data` module as follows,

```
import skimage.data as data
img = data.astronaut()
io.imshow(img)
io.show()
```

The code above shows the image of astronaut **Eileen Collins** (https://en.wikipedia.org/wiki/Eileen_Collins), a retired **NASA** astronaut.

We can use `imread()`, `imshow()`, and `show()` from **matplotlib** too to display images as follows,

```
import matplotlib.pyplot as plt
img = data.coffee()
plt.imshow(img)
plt.title('Coffee')
```

```
plt.axis('off')
plt.show()
```

In case, you want to generate your own test data and use it as an image, which is also possible. Scikit-image has `binary_blob()` functions that allows us to generate binary test data, as follows, *(figure 10.1)*

```
img = data.binary_blobs(length=512, blob_size_
fraction=0.1, seed=5)
io.imshow(img)
io.show()
```

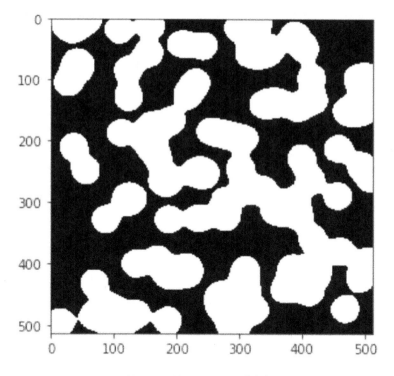

Figure 10.1 Binary blob

10.4 Colorspace Conversion

A **color model** is mathematical way of describing colors. Colorspaces map real life colors to the values in the color models. The `imread()` function of most of the image processing libraries read the images and stores them with **RGB** as colorspace. Many times, we need to change the colorspace of an image for image processing. **Scikit-image** has functions to change the colorspace of images. Let's see the demonstration. We will use the `color` module that has all the functions to convert colorspace.

```
from skimage.color import convert_colorspace
```

Let's choose astronaut image for the demo,

```
img = data.astronaut()
plt.imshow(img)
plt.show()
```

Following code converts the image from RGB to HSV colorspace,

```
img_hsv = convert_colorspace(img, 'RGB', 'HSV')
plt.imshow(img_hsv)
plt.show()
```

We can even convert **RGB** image into greyscale using `rgb2grey()` or `rgb2gray()` functions as follows,

```
from skimage.color import rgb2gray, rgb2grey
img_gray = rgb2gray(img)
plt.imshow(img_gray, cmap = 'gray')
plt.show()
```

10.5 Summary

In this brief and short chapter, we studies how to get started with **scikit image**. We have learned how to install it on Windows and Raspberry Pi platforms. We, also, have studied the basic functions and colorspace conversion. From the next chapter onwards, we will study more advanced functionalities offered by **scikit-image**.

Exercise

Generate various test images with `binary_blob()` function. Visit https://scikit-image.org/ for more information about scikit-image library.

CHAPTER 11

Thresholding Histogram Equalization and Transformations

In the last chapter, we have learned the basics of the scikit-image. We, also, have learned how to access the images in the data module and how to create custom images for testing with `binary_blob()`.

We have, already, learned the concept of thresholding with **NumPy**. In this chapter, we will observe the same concept once again. Additionally, we will learn how to equalize image histogram to enhance the quality of images. Also, we will acquire the knowledge of how to transform images.

11.1 Simple Thresholding, Otsu's Binarization, and Adaptive Thresholding

We have already seen how to implement simple **thresholding**. In this section, we will implement the same using different style and by using `data` module from scikit-image library. Following is the code for that,

```
%matplotlib inline
import matplotlib.pyplot as plt
import skimage.data as data

img = data.camera()

thresh = 127

output1 = img > thresh
output2 = img <= thresh

output = [img, output1, output2]
```

```
titles = ['Original', 'Thresholded', 'Inverted
Threshold']

for i in range(3):
    plt.subplot(1, 3, i+1)
    plt.imshow(output[i], cmap='gray')
    plt.title(titles[i])
    plt.axis('off')

plt.show()            .
```

The output of above program will be thresholded image and inverted thresholded image. We are using `data.camera()`, as our test image. Revising the logic for thresholding was important. Here, we're deciding the threshold value ourselves. We can have the threshold calculated by the custom algorithms. One of such algorithms is **Otsu's Binarization**. It is named after its inventor **Nobuyuki Otsu** (https://en.wikipedia.org/wiki/Nobuyuki_Otsu). In this algorithm, the **threshold** of an image is automatically computed. This is the best way to threshold images with bimodal histogram. **Bimodal histogram** is a histogram with two peaks. In such images, there are usually foreground and background areas. After thresholding, we can easily label foreground and background areas. Scikit-image has `threshold_otsu()` function to compute the threshold for an image. Following is the code example of the same,

```
from skimage.filters import threshold_otsu
thresh = threshold_otsu(img)
binary = img > thresh
plt.subplots_adjust(wspace=0.5, hspace=0.5)
plt.subplot(1, 3, 1)
plt.title('Original Image')
plt.imshow(img, cmap='gray')
plt.axis('off')
plt.subplot(1, 3, 2)
plt.title('Bimodal histogram')
plt.hist(img.ravel(), bins=256, range=[0, 255])
plt.xlim([0, 255])
plt.subplot(1, 3, 3)
plt.title('Thresholded Image')
plt.imshow(binary, cmap='gray')
```

```
plt.axis('off')
plt.show()
```

Following is the output, original image with bimodal histogram and thresholded image, *(figure 11.1)*

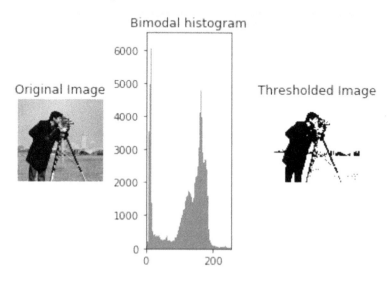

Figure 11.1 Bimodal histogram and otsu's binarization

In the earlier examples, the threshold was computed for entire image. In adaptive thresholding, threshold is computed region-wise. So, each region has different threshold. In **scikit-image**, we provide the block size and offset. Following is a sample program that calculates the thresholded image using adaptive thresholding,

```
from skimage.filters import threshold_local
img = data.page()
adaptive = threshold_local(img, block_size = 3, offset
= 30)
plt.imshow(adaptive, cmap='gray')
plt.show()
```

Following is the output, *(figure 11.2)*

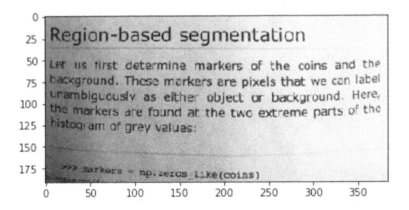

Figure 11.2 Adaptive thresholding

11.2 Histogram Equalization

We know that histogram is representation of distribution of intensities of a channel in an image. Histogram equalization is the process of adjusting the intensities in histogram such that we get the contrast of an image enhanced. **Scikit-image** has function `equalize_hist()` and `equalize_adapthist()` to perform histogram equalization. The following program demonstrates the usage of both the functions,

```
%matplotlib inline
import matplotlib.pyplot as plt
from skimage import data
from skimage import exposure
img = data.moon()
img_eq = exposure.equalize_hist(img)
img_adapthist = exposure.equalize_adapthist(img, clip_
limit=0.03)
output = [img, img_eq, img_adapthist]
titles = ['Original', 'Histogram Equalization',
'Adaptive Equalization']
for i in range(3):
    plt.subplot(3, 1, i+1)
    plt.imshow(output[i], cmap='gray')
    plt.title(titles[i])
    plt.axis('off')
plt.show()
```

The output is as follows, *(figure 11.3)*

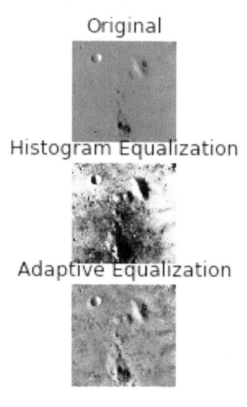

Figure 11.3 Histogram Equalization

11.3 Image Transformations

Transformations means change in the form or appearance. We are going to study a few transformations on images in this section. The first transformation, we will see, is similarity transform. It is a type of geometric transformation. In similarity transform angles and ratios between distances is preserved. Scikit-image function `SimilarityTransform()` can calculate the object for similarity transformation by providing it scale, rotation, and translation. Then, we can use `warp()` function to apply this object on image to compute the transformed image.

First, we import all the required libraries and images, as follows,

```
%matplotlib inline
import math
import numpy as np
import matplotlib.pyplot as plt
from skimage import data
from skimage import transform as tf
img = data.astronaut()
```

The following is the program for computing rotation, scaling, and translation operations with similarity transformation. We are, also, computing the inverse transformation in the same example,

```
# Similarity Transform
tform = tf.SimilarityTransform(scale=1, rotation=math.
pi/4,
translation=(img.shape[0]/2, -100))
print(tform)
output1 = tf.warp(img, tform)
output2 = tf.warp(img, tform.inverse)
output = [img, output1, output2]
titles = ['Original', '45 Degrees counter-clockwise',
'45 Degrees clockwise']
plt.subplots_adjust(wspace=0.5, hspace=0.5)
for i in range(3):
    plt.subplot(3, 1, i+1)
    plt.imshow(output[i])
    plt.title(titles[i])
    plt.xticks([]), plt.yticks([])
plt.show()
```

Following is the output of the program above, *(figure 11.4)*

Original

45 Degrees counter-clockwise

45 Degrees clockwise

Figure 11.4 Similarity Transform and Inverse Similarity Transform

We can move the water in a vessel in twisting or spinning motion. This effect is known as **swirl**. Think about the whirlpool effect in the water. We can apply the same effect on images also. Scikit-image has `swirl()` function that accepts rotation, strength, and radius for the swirl effect on image. Following is the example of the swirl effect,

```
output1 = tf.swirl(img, rotation=50, strength=10,
radius=120, mode='reflect')
output2 = tf.swirl(img, rotation=10, strength=20,
radius=200, mode='reflect')
output = [img, output1, output2]
titles = ['Original', 'Swirl 1', 'Swirl 2']
for i in range(3):
    plt.subplot(1, 3, i+1)
    plt.imshow(output[i], interpolation='nearest')
    plt.title(titles[i])
    plt.xticks([]), plt.yticks([])
plt.show()
```

Following is the output, *(figure 11.5)*

Figure 11.5 Swirl Transform

Let's see the **projective transformation**. The projective transformation shows how the perceived objects change when the view point of the observer changes. This transformation allows creating the distortion of the perspective for the observer. It does not preserve parallelism, lengths, and angles of lines between input and output image. However, it still preserves **collinearity** and **incidence**. Following is an example of projective transformation,

```
# Projective Transform
img = data.text()
src = np.array([[0, 0], [0, 50], [300, 50], [300, 0]])
dst = np.array([[155, 15], [65, 40], [260, 130], [360, 95]])

tform = tf.ProjectiveTransform()
tform.estimate(src, dst)
output1 = tf.warp(img, tform, output_shape=(50, 300))
output = [img, output1]
titles = ['Original', 'Projective Transform']
for i in range(2):
    plt.subplot(1, 2, i+1)
    plt.imshow(output[i], cmap='gray')
    plt.title(titles[i])
    plt.xticks([]), plt.yticks([])
plt.show()
```

The output is as follows, *(figure 11.6)*

Original

Projective Transform

Figure 11.6 Projective Transform

Now, let's see the affine transformation which is special case of projective transform. Unlike the affine transformation, the parallelism between the lines is preserved. The function `AffineTransform()` accepts scale, rotation, sheer, and translation as arguments and returns transform object which can be applied on the image with `warp()` function as follows,

```
img = data.checkerboard()
tform = tf.AffineTransform(scale=(1.2, 1.1),
rotation=1, shear=0.7,
translation=(210, 50))
output1 = tf.warp(img, tform, output_shape=(350, 350))
output2 = tf.warp(img, tform.inverse, output_
shape=(350, 350))
output = [img, output1, output2]
titles = ['Original', 'Affine', 'Inverse Affine']
for i in range(3):
    plt.subplot(1, 3, i+1)
    plt.imshow(output[i], cmap='gray')
    plt.xticks([]), plt.yticks([])
    plt.title(titles[i])
plt.show()
```

We have applied the transformation on a checkerboard (or chessboard) image. Note that, the angles between the lines change in the output yet the parallelism between the lines is preserved. Following is the output, *(figure 11.7)*

Figure 11.7 Affine Transform

In the affine and similarity transforms, we can scale the images. Scaling operation scales the images in the same proportion for X and Y axes. We can independently scale the axes of an image with `resize()` function. Let's see an example of the same,

```
img = data.coffee()
output1 = tf.resize(img, (img.shape[0], img.shape[1] *
1/2), mode='reflect')
plt.subplots_adjust(wspace=0.5, hspace=0.5)
output = [img, output1]
titles = ['Original', 'Resized Image']
for i in range(2):
    plt.subplot(2, 1, i+1)
    plt.imshow(output[i])
    plt.title(titles[i])
plt.show()
```

Following is the output, *(figure 11.8)*

Figure 11.8 Resize Transform

As you can see, we have resized the image in X axis only.

11.4 Summary

In this very brief chapter, we studied various types of **transformations** in detail and implemented the same on various images. In the next chapter, we will study the concept of **image filtering** and apply various types of filters on images.

Exercise

As an exercise to this chapter, you can alter the values of arguments passed to various parameters in the functions we have used in this chapter.

CHAPTER 12
Kernels, Convolution and Filters

In the last chapter, we have learned a few important image processing concepts like thresholding, histogram equalization, and transforms with scikit-image. In this chapter, we will study the concepts of image kernels and filters, in detail. We will learn how we can enhance a few qualities of an image by using different types of image filters.

12.1 Image Filtering

The process of enhancing image features is known as **image filtering**. We can use convolution operation to filter images. We need a kernel for convolution operation. A **kernel** or a **convolution matrix** is a small matrix that is used for a variety of operations on images. Depending on the kernel, we get the output after convolution. Various filters use different types of kernels to achieve image filtering effect. There are two types of filters, one is, high pass filters and another is, low pass filters. **High pass filters** allow high frequency parts of image like edges to pass. High pass filters are used for sharpening and edge detection. **Low pass filters** allow low frequency components of image to pass through them. They can produce blur effect or remove noise from image. In this section, we will see how to create our own custom filters with signal processing routine in **SciPy** library.

Create a new **Jupyter** notebook. Import the `signal` module from **SciPy** library and other libraries, as follows:

```
from scipy import signal
import numpy as np
from skimage import data
from matplotlib import pyplot as plt
```

Load the camera image into a variable,

```
img = data.camera()
```

The function `convolve2d()` convolves two 2-D matrices. One of the **matrices** is the image matrix and another matrix is the kernel. Let's see the code,

```
kernel = np.ones((3, 3),np.float32)/9
dst2 = signal.convolve2d(img, kernel, boundary='symm',
mode='same')
plt.imshow(dst2, cmap='gray')
plt.show()
```

In the code above, the **kernel** is a unit 3x3 matrix divided by 9. This creates simple blur effect, *(figure 12.1)*

Figure 12.1 Simple Blur Kernel (3x3)

We can also increase size of the kernel as follows,

```
# Simple Blur
kernel = np.ones((7, 7),np.float32)/49
dst2 = signal.convolve2d(img, kernel, boundary='symm',
mode='same')
plt.imshow(dst2, cmap='gray')
plt.show()
```

Bigger kernel causes stronger blur effect, *(figure 12.2)*

Figure 12.2 Simple Blur Kernel (7x7)

We can also achieve box blur with the following kernel,

```
# Box blur
kernel = np.array([[0.0625, 0.125, 0.0625],
                   [0.125, 0.25, 0.125],
                   [0.0625, 0.125, 0.0625]])
dst2 = signal.convolve2d(img, kernel, boundary='symm',
mode='same')
plt.imshow(dst2, cmap='gray')
plt.show()
```

Run the program above and check the result.

All the above kernels were low-pass filter kernels. That's why, they produced image smoothing or blur effect. Let's see a couple of high-pass filter kernels. First example is the kernel used for image sharpening,

```
# Sharpen
kernel = np.array([[0, -1, 0],
                   [-1, 5, -1],
                   [0, -1, 0]])
```

```
dst2 = signal.convolve2d(img, kernel, boundary='symm',
mode='same')
plt.imshow(dst2, cmap='gray')
plt.show()
```

The output is as follows, *(figure 12.3)*

Figure 12.3 Image Sharpen Kernel (3x3)

We can even detect edges with a high-pass kernel, as follows,

```
# Edge Detection
kernel = np.array([[-1, -1, -1],
                   [-1, 8, -1],
                   [-1, -1,-1]])

dst2 = signal.convolve2d(img, kernel, boundary='symm',
mode='same')

plt.imshow(dst2, cmap='gray')
plt.show()
```

Following is the output, *(figure 12.4)*

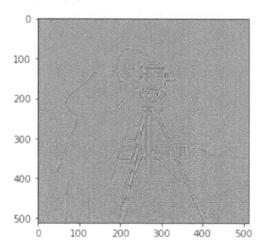

Figure 12.4 Edge detection Kernel

12.2 Built-in Image Filters in Scikit-image

Scikit-image has many built-in image filters. We will see plenty of examples of these filters in this section. The first filter is **Gaussian filter**. It is a very useful filter that can filter the Gaussian noise from and image. Following is the code example,

```
%matplotlib inline
from skimage.data import camera
from skimage.filters import gaussian
from matplotlib import pyplot as plt
img = camera()
out1 = gaussian(img, sigma=2)

output = [img, out1]

titles = ['Original', 'Gaussian']

for i in range(2):
    plt.subplot(1, 2, i+1)
```

```
    plt.title(titles[i])
    plt.imshow(output[i], cmap='gray')
    plt.xticks([]), plt.yticks([])
plt.show()
```

Run the code and see the output.

We also have **Laplacian filter** that can highlight the edges,

```
from skimage.filters import laplace
out1 = laplace(img, ksize=3)
output = [img, out1]
titles = ['Original', 'Laplacian']
for i in range(2):
    plt.subplot(1, 2, i+1)
    plt.title(titles[i])
    plt.imshow(output[i], cmap='gray')
    plt.xticks([]), plt.yticks([])
plt.show()
```

We, also, have **Prewitt filter** to highlight the edge in the image,

```
from skimage.filters import prewitt_h, prewitt_v,
prewitt

out1 = prewitt_h(img)
out2 = prewitt_v(img)
out3 = prewitt(img)

output = [img, out1, out2, out3]
titles = ['Original', 'Prewitt Horizontal', 'Prewitt
Vertical', 'Prewitt']

for i in range(4):
    plt.subplot(2, 2, i+1)
    plt.title(titles[i])
    plt.imshow(output[i], cmap='gray')
    plt.xticks([]), plt.yticks([])
plt.show()
```

We also have **Scharr filter** to highlight edges,

```
from skimage.filters import scharr_h, scharr_v, scharr


out1 = scharr_h(img)
out2 = scharr_v(img)
out3 = scharr(img)

output = [img, out1, out2, out3]
titles = ['Original', 'Scharr Horizontal', 'Scharr
Vertical', 'Scharr']

for i in range(4):
    plt.subplot(2, 2, i+1)
    plt.title(titles[i])
    plt.imshow(output[i], cmap='gray')
    plt.xticks([]), plt.yticks([])
plt.show()
```

Run all the programs above and check the output.

If you have noticed, we have used a greyscale image for all these operations. We have to write custom code for all these filters to work with **RGB** images. Following is the example of the custom code for Scharr filter,

```
%matplotlib inline
from skimage.color.adapt_rgb import adapt_rgb, each_
channel, hsv_value
from skimage import filters
from skimage import data
from skimage.exposure import rescale_intensity
import matplotlib.pyplot as plt
@adapt_rgb(each_channel)
def scharr_each(image):
    return filters.scharr(image)

@adapt_rgb(hsv_value)
def scharr_hsv(image):
```

```
        return filters.scharr(image)
```

```
image = data.coffee()
out1 = rescale_intensity(1 - scharr_each(image))
out2 = rescale_intensity(1 - scharr_hsv(image))
```

In the code above, we are creating two custom functions with `@adapt_rgb()` decorator. The function `scharr_each()` will split image to red, green, and blue channels and then it will apply the filter to those channels separately. Then, all the channels will be recombined to form the filtered image. Following code demonstrates that,

```
plt.imshow(out1)
plt.show()
```

Following is the output, *(figure 12.5)*

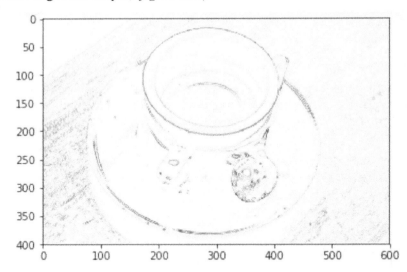

Figure 12.5 Output of Scharr filter applied on RGB channels separately

The function `scharr_hsv()` will split convert **RGB** image to **HSV** image. Then, it will split image to hue, saturation, and value components and then it will apply the filter to those components separately. Then, all the combined will be recombined to form the filtered image. Following code demonstrates that,

```
plt.imshow(out2)
plt.show()
```

Following is the output, *(figure 12.6)*

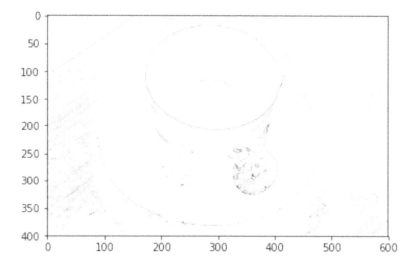

Figure 12.6 Output of Scharr filter applied on HSV components separately

12.3 Summary

In this chapter, we have explored the concepts of kernels, convolution, and filters. In the next chapter we will study morphological operations. We will also see how to restore damaged images.

Exercise

Scikit-image has more filters. Write code to call the functions for Robers, Sobel, Frangi, and Hessian filters. Check https://scikit-image.org/docs/dev/api/skimage.filters.html for reference.

CHAPTER 13

Morphological Operations and Image Restoration

In the last chapter, we studied image filters in great details. First, we started with the definitions of filters and kernels. Then, we implemented many filters ourselves and we used the filters available in the scikit-image.

In this chapter, we will study the concept of morphological operations and image restoration in detail.

13.1 Mathematical Morphology and Morphological Operations

Mathematical morphology (MM) is a technique for the analysis and processing of spatial structures like graphs, surface meshes, solids, and many other spatial structures. We can use morphological techniques (or operations) on digital images too. There are four very useful morphological techniques that can be used with digital images. Those are erosion, dilation, opening, and closing. We can use these operations with binary, greyscale, and color images. Just as we need a kernel matrix for filtering, we need a matrix called **structuring element** for morphological operations. Structuring element is a matrix that holds a shape which is used to interact with given image. Scikit-image provides a lot of shapes for structuring elements. Following are the examples:

```
%matplotlib inline
from skimage import morphology
import numpy as np
print(morphology.square(4, np.uint8))
print('\n')
```

The output is as follows:

```
[[1.  1.]
 [1.  1.]
 [1.  1.]
 [1.  1.]
 [1.  1.]
 [1.  1.]]
```

Run the following examples of structuring elements and check the result:

```
print(morphology.rectangle(6, 2, np.float16))
print('\n')
print(morphology.diamond(4, np.float16))
print('\n')
print(morphology.disk(4, np.float16))
print('\n')
print(morphology.cube(4, np.float16))
print('\n')
print(morphology.octahedron(4, np.float16))
print('\n')
print(morphology.ball(3, np.float16))
print('\n')
print(morphology.octagon(3, 4, np.float16))
print('\n')
print(morphology.star(4, np.float16))
print('\n')
```

We will see how to use these structuring elements for morphological operations.

Let's understand the meaning of various morphological operations. **Erosion** will contract the darker parts and will expand lighter parts of an image. **Dilation** is reverse of erosion. It expands lighter parts and contract the darker parts. Erosion followed by dilation is Opening. Dilation followed by erosion is **Closing**. It is difficult to understand the meanings of these operations. Best way is to apply all these on a binary image for better understanding.

```
from skimage import data
import matplotlib.pyplot as plt
image = out1 = out2 = out3 = out4 = data.horse()
plt.imshow(image, cmap='gray')
```

```
plt.show()
```

The output is as follows: *(figure 13.1)*

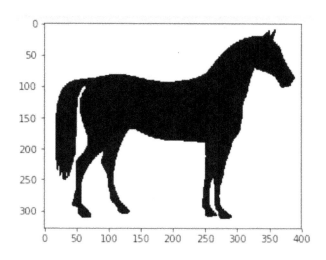

Figure 13.1 Binary image for testing

Apply all the morphological operations on the image for 20 times, as follows:

```
for i in range(20):
    out1 = morphology.binary_erosion(out1)
    out2 = morphology.binary_dilation(out2)

    out3 = morphology.binary_opening(out3)
    out4 = morphology.binary_closing(out4)
```

Let's visualize the erosion:

```
plt.imshow(out1, cmap='gray')
plt.show()
```

The output is, as follows: *(figure 13.2)*

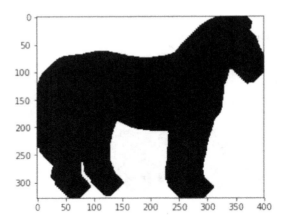

Figure 13.2 Erosion

The visualization of dilation is, as follows:

```
plt.imshow(out2, cmap='gray')
plt.show()
```

The output is as follows: *(figure 13.3)*

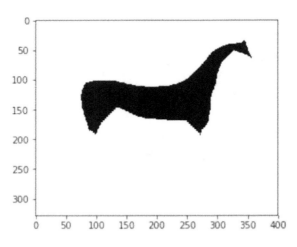

Figure 13.3 Erosion

Visualize the erosion and dilation too.

In the earlier example, we saw the binary morphological operation. We just passed the binary image array to all the morphological functions. In that case, the default structuring element is a cross shaped element. Following is an example of a custom element and erosion operation.

```
selem = morphology.star(4, np.float16)
output = morphology.binary_erosion(data.horse(),selem)
plt.imshow(output, cmap='gray')
plt.show()
```

Run the above code and see the output. In the same way, we can perform other binary morphological operations with other custom structuring elements.

We can even apply morphological operations on greyscale image and we have nob-binary versions of morphological functions as follows:

```
image = out1 = out2 = out3 = out4 = data.camera()
for i in range(20):

    out1 = morphology.erosion(out1)
    out2 = morphology.dilation(out2)
    out3 = morphology.opening(out3)
    out4 = morphology.closing(out4)
```

We can also use the same functions for color images:

```
image = out1 = out2 = out3 = out4 = data.coffee()
for i in range(20):
    out1 = morphology.erosion(out1)
    out2 = morphology.dilation(out2)
    out3 = morphology.opening(out3)
    out4 = morphology.closing(out4)
```

Run both the code snippets and write the code for visualizing outputs after the execution of each of them.

13.2 Image Restoration by Inpainting

Image restoration is process of restoring damaged images. We are going to explore inpainting in this section. In inpainting, we estimate the pixels in the damaged part and restore them. Let's see how we can do that with scikit-image step by step:

```
%matplotlib inline
import numpy as np
import matplotlib.pyplot as plt

from skimage import data
from skimage.restoration import inpaint
image = data.coffee()[0:200, 0:200]
plt.imshow(image)
plt.show()
```

In the code above, we are taking 200x200 section of coffee mug image. Now let's create a defect mask:

```
# Create mask with three defect regions: left, middle,
right respectively
mask = np.zeros(image.shape[:-1])
mask[20:60, 0:20] = 1
mask[160:180, 70:155] = 1
mask[30:60, 170:195] = 1
plt.imshow(mask, cmap='gray')
plt.show()
```

Following is the output: *(figure 13.4)*

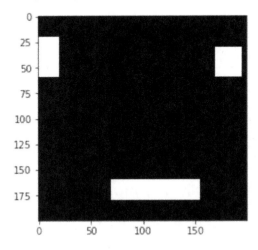

Figure 13.4 Image Mask

We can apply inverted image defect mask on the image as follows:

```
defect = image.copy()
for layer in range(defect.shape[-1]):
    defect[np.where(mask)] = 0
plt.imshow(defect)
plt.show()
```

Following is the output: *(figure 13.5)*

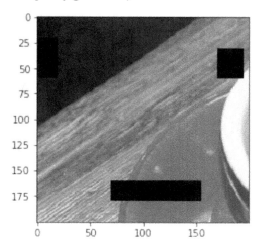

Figure 13.5 Defect mask applied on image

We can apply the inpainting function:

```
result = inpaint.inpaint_biharmonic(defect, mask,
multichannel=True)
plt.imshow(result)
plt.show()
```

Following is the restored image: *(figure 13.6)*

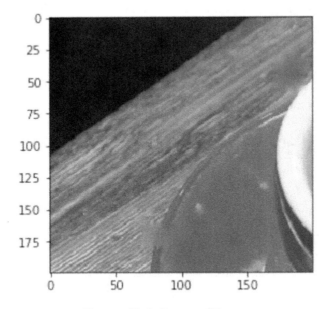

Figure 13.6 Restored Image

This is how we can restore a damaged image.

13.3 Summary

In this chapter, we studied morphological operations and image inpainting. In the next chapter, we will have look at edge detection.

CHAPTER 14

Noise Removal and Edge Detection

In the last chapter, studied **morphological operations** on binary, greyscale, and color images. We have, also, learned the associated concept of **structuring element matrix**. We have finished the chapter with the concept and demonstration of **image restoration**.

In this chapter, we will study the concept of **noise**, in detail. We will also see the demonstration of a few noise removal techniques on a noisy image sample. We will, then, see the canny method of edge detection.

14.1 Noise

Information is represented in terms of signals. Any unwanted disturbance in the signals is **noise**. And any unwanted disturbance in the electronic signals is **electronic noise**. **Image noise** is an aspect of electronic noise. In digital images, the **noise** is introduced by electronic circuitry of either digital camera or photo/film scanner. In analog images, the **noise** is introduced due to the film grain, and it is further replicated to digital images when analog images/films are scanned to the digital format. **Image noise** is random variation in the intensity of the pixels in the digital image. **Signal-to-Noise Ratio** is defined as the ratio of signal power to the noise power. It is one of the ways, we measure the **noise**.

There are many types of **noise** like Gaussian noise, salt-and-pepper noise, etc. Let's see the demonstrations of random noise first, as follow:

```
%matplotlib inline
import numpy as np
import matplotlib.pyplot as plt
```

```
import random
from skimage import data, img_as_float
from skimage.util import random_noise
original = img_as_float(data.astronaut())
sigma = 0.155
noisy = random_noise(original, var=sigma**2)
plt.imshow(noisy)
plt.axis('off')
plt.show()
```

The image with random noise, as follows: *(figure 14.1)*

Figure 14.1 Image with random noise

We will see how to add salt-and-pepper noise to an image. When we randomly add black and white pixels to an image, then it is **salt-and-pepper noise**. Let's create an empty image, as follows:

```
s_a_p_noisy = np.zeros(original.shape, np.float64)
```

We add either image pixels or salt (white pixels) or pepper (black pixels) based on the values of variables p and r. Following is the code:

```
p = 0.1
```

```
for i in range(original.shape[0]):
    for j in range(original.shape[1]):
        r = random.random()
        if r < p/2:
            s_a_p_noisy[i][j] = 0.0, 0.0, 0.0
        elif r < p:
            s_a_p_noisy[i][j] = 255.0, 255.0, 255.0
        else:
            s_a_p_noisy[i][j] = original[i][j]
plt.imshow(s_a_p_noisy)
plt.axis('off')
plt.show()
```

Following is the output, *(figure 14.2)*

Figure 14.2 Image with salt and pepper noise

14.2 Noise Removal

There are many functions implemented in scikit-image for noise removal. Let's see a demo of usage of all the noise removal functions. Following is the code example:

```
%matplotlib inline
import numpy as np
import matplotlib.pyplot as plt
```

```
from skimage.restoration import (denoise_tv_chambolle,
denoise_bilateral, denoise_nl_means, denoise_tv_
bregman)
from skimage import data, img_as_float
from skimage.util import random_noise
original = img_as_float(data.astronaut()[0:100, 0:100])
plt.imshow(original)
plt.show()
```

The program, above, will show the 100x100 part of astronaut image. Let's **add noise** to that:

```
sigma = 0.155
noisy = random_noise(original, var=sigma**2)
plt.imshow(noisy)
plt.show()
```

Let's apply a **denoising** function on the noisy imag:e

```
output1 = denoise_tv_chambolle(noisy, weight=0.1,
multichannel=True)
plt.imshow(output1)
plt.show()
```

Bilateral denoising function too cleans the noise considerably:

```
output2 = denoise_bilateral(noisy, sigma_color=0.05,
sigma_spatial=15, multichannel=True)
plt.imshow(output2)
plt.show()
```

NL means denoising, as follows:

```
output3 = denoise_nl_means(noisy, multichannel=True)
plt.imshow(output3)
plt.show()
```

Another **denoising** function, as follows:

```
output4 = denoise_tv_bregman(noisy, weight=2)
plt.imshow(output4)
plt.show()
```

Run the above code snippets, in the different cells of a new **Jupyter** notebook, and check the output.

14.3 Canny Edge Detector

Canny Edge Detector is an edge detector algorithm. It works in multiple stages. It is named after its developer **John F Canny**. The Canny Edge Detection has following stages:

1. Smooth image by removing the noise by applying Gaussian filter.
2. Calculate the intensity gradients of the image.
3. Apply non-maximum suppression.
4. Apply double threshold to calculate all the potential edges.
5. Finalize the edges by removing all the edges that are not connected to strong edges.

Scikit-image has a function **canny()** that computes the edges in the images. Let's see the example code:

```
%matplotlib inline
import numpy as np
import matplotlib.pyplot as plt
from skimage import feature, data
original = data.camera()
plt.imshow(original, cmap='gray')
plt.axis('off')
plt.show()
```

The code above shows the cameraman image. Let's apply Canny edge detection function, as follows:

```
edges1 = feature.canny(original)
# by default sigma = 1
plt.imshow(edges1, cmap='gray')
plt.axis('off')
plt.show()
```

Following is the result of edges in the image, *(Figure 14.3)*

Figure 14.3 Edges in the cameraman image

14.4 Summary

In this chapter, we have studied noise, noise removal, and edge detection. In the next chapter, we will study some more advanced image processing concepts.

Exercise

Run the **Canny edge detection program** with different values of the parameter sigma. Following is the example:

```
edges1 = feature.canny(original, sigma=3)
```

CHAPTER 15
Advanced Image Processing Operations

In the last chapter, we studied the concept of noise, signal-to-noise ratio, and denoising of images. We also learned how to detect edges in an image with **Canny edge detection algorithm**.

In this chapter, we will have a look at the advanced concepts in the image processing domain and their implementation with **scikit-image** and **matplotlib**.

15.1 SLIC Segmentation

Segmentation means dividing the image into distinct regions based on the similarities between pixels. There are many methods of segmenting images. **Simple Linear Iterative Clustering (SLIC)** performs a local clustering of pixels in the 5-D space, defined by the L, a, b values of the CIELAB color space and the x, y pixel coordinates. The **SLIC** Superpixels technique was proposed by **Radhakrishna Achanta, Appu Shaji, Kevin Smith, Aurelien Lucchi, Pascal Fua,** and **Sabine Susstrunk** at **EPFL** in **June 2010**. Following is the implementation of it with scikit-image:

```
%matplotlib inline
from skimage import data, segmentation, color
from skimage.future import graph
from matplotlib import pyplot as plt

img = data.coffee()

labels = segmentation.slic(img, compactness=30, n_
segments=1000)
```

```
out = color.label2rgb(labels, img, kind='avg')

plt.imshow(out)
plt.axis('off')
plt.show()
```

The output is as follows: *(figure 15.1)*

Figure 15.1 SLIC Segmentation Demo

You can find the relevant paper at http://www.kev-smith.com/papers/ SLIC_Superpixels.pdf.

15.2 Tinting Greyscale Images

We can apply shades of various colors to the greyscale images. For that first, we need to convert the single channel greyscale image to a RGB image. Note that, we are just changing the colorspace of the image, not the data related to the color information. Following is the code example:

```
%matplotlib inline
import matplotlib.pyplot as plt
from skimage import data, color, img_as_float
grayscale_image = img_as_float(data.moon()[::2, ::2])
image = color.gray2rgb(grayscale_image)
plt.imshow(image)
plt.show()
```

Let's define a multiplier and multiply the image array with that. Following is the example, how we can apply red tint to the image:

```
red_multiplier = [1, 0, 0]
output1 = image * red_multiplier
plt.imshow(output1)
plt.show()
```

By changing the values of the multiplier array, we can create various tints, as follows:

```
green_multiplier = [0, 1, 0]
blue_multiplier = [0, 0, 1]
yellow_multiplier = [1, 1, 0]
cyan_multiplier = [0, 1, 1]
```

Try to create more **tint arrays**.

15.3 Contours

A **contours** is a curve joining all the continuous points, along the boundary, that have same color (for color images) or intensity (for greyscale images). The applications of contour are **shape analysis** and **object detection**. Let's see an example of contour, as follows:

```
%matplotlib inline
import numpy as np
import matplotlib.pyplot as plt
from skimage import measure
x, y = np.ogrid[-np.pi:np.pi:100j, -np.pi:np.pi:100j]
r = np.cos(np.exp((np.sin(x)**3 + np.cos(y)**5)))

# Display the image and plot all contours found
plt.imshow(r, interpolation='nearest')
# Find contours at a constant value of 0.8
contours = measure.find_contours(r, 0.8)
for n, contour in enumerate(contours):
    plt.plot(contour[:, 1], contour[:, 0],
linewidth=2)
plt.title('Contours')
plt.axis('off')
plt.show()
```

The output looks, as follows: *(figure 15.2)*

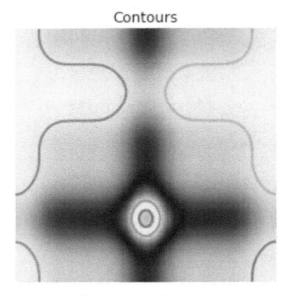

Figure 15.2 Contours

15.4 Summary

In this chapter, we have studied contours, SLIC segmentation, and tinting greyscale images. In the next chapter, we will study about the various distributions of Python and **Anaconda distribution**.

CHAPTER 16

Wrapping Up

In the last chapter, we have covered advanced operations on images with **scikit-image**. We have covered all the image processing concepts intended to be covered in this book, till now. In this chapter, we will learn a few important things, which we have not covered in the earlier chapters. Readers will find these topics very useful while working in the real life projects. We will understand various distributions of **Python** and **conda** package manager.

16.1 Python Implementations and Distributions

The implementation of **Python** that we worked with till now (the one downloaded from **Python** Software Foundation's website and also available with **Raspberry Pi Raspbian**) is called **CPython**. It is known by the name because it has been implemented in **C programming language**. There are other implementations and distributions of **Python** programming language. We can find the list of these implementations and distributions at https://wiki.python.org/moin/PythonDistributions and https://www.python.org/download/alternatives/. We are going to see the **Anaconda** distribution of **Python** in detail in this chapter. We will learn how to install **Anaconda** on Windows OS. We will also see the details of **conda** package manager.

16.2 Anaconda

Anaconda is a popular **Python** distribution that is widely used by the individuals and organizations involved in scientific computing with **Python**. We can download the installer from https://www.anaconda.com/distribution/. Once downloaded, you can find it in the **Downloads** directory for your user in Windows. Launch the installation wizard and make sure that you check the box to add **Anaconda** to system PATH environment variable, *(figure 16.1)*

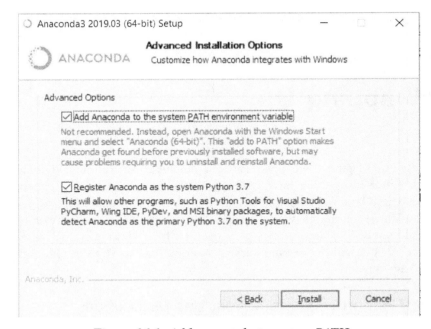

Figure 16.1 Add anaconda to system PATH

It takes quite a while to install **Anaconda** as it has many packages bundled with it. We can see the list of packages that come with **Anaconda** https://docs.anaconda.com/anaconda/packages/pkg-docs/.

16.3 Conda Package Manager

Conda is a package manager and environment management system like pip. The main difference between **pip** and **conda** is **conda** is package manager for many other programming languages like R too. **Conda** comes with **Anaconda** by default. You can also install **conda** separately with pip.

Run the following command, on **Raspberry Pi,** to install **conda**:

```
sudo pip3 install conda
```

Once **conda** is installed, we can **update** it with the following command:

```
conda update conda
```

The following command, shows us the **version**:

```
conda -V
```

We can see the **list of installed packages**, with the subsequent command:

```
conda list
```

We can **search** for a package in the **conda** repository, with the following command:

```
conda search opecv
```

We can **install** a package from the **conda** repository, with the following command:

```
conda install opencv
```

We can **uninstall** a package using **conda,** with the following command:

```
conda uninstall opencv
```

16.4 Spyder IDE

Anaconda comes with an IDE known as **Spyder IDE**. **Spyder** has an **integrated IPython interactive prompt**. You can search for it by typing in **Spyder,** in the Windows search bar.

In the *figure 16.2*, on the left, we can see the code editor. In the bottom right corner, we have interactive **IPython** prompt where we can see the output of the execution of a **Python** program.

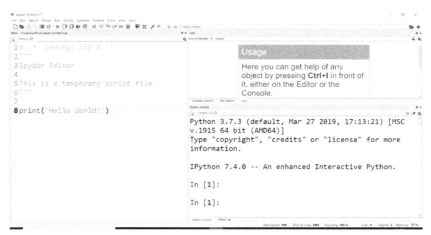

Figure 16.2 Screenshot of Spyder IDE

16.5 Summary

In this chapter, we have learned a few important topics like **conda package manager** and **Anaconda** distribution of **Python**.

16.6 Conclusion

In this book, initially we have learned basics of **Python** and then we, just, moved on to exploring **Jupyter** notebook environment. For any type of scientific computing, **NumPy** is the fundamental library to be explored, so we explored the same. Then, we saw image processing with **NumPy** and **matplotlib**. Finally, learned many image processing concepts in detail with scikit-image. In the end, we have learned how to use **conda** package manager and how to install **Anaconda** distribution of **Python**.

This book gives us the adequate information about image processing concept. All the programming examples, combined with exercises, provide us a very good and in-depth understanding of important image processing techniques. You can now, further explore the world of scientific computing with **Python,** by studying other important libraries like **SciPy** and **OpenCV**. Happy exploring and learning!

Code Bundle

All the code samples used in the book can be found at the following github repository:

https://github.com/bpbpublications/Python-3-Image-Processing

www.ingramcontent.com/pod-product-compliance
Lightning Source LLC
LaVergne TN
LVHW022316060326
832902LV00020B/3499